WHY THE FUCK NOT?

DAVID L. LITVIN

CONTENTS

FOREWORD

Few will remember an American singer-songwriter from a half century ago named Emitt Rhodes. He released a few minor, now forgotten hits in the early 1970s. In fact, he ended up better-known for the short recitation on his self-titled debut album cover than any of the songs contained thereon when he intrepidly pronounced:

"I want to say what I feel, and feel what I say."

In those ten short words, Emitt Rhodes perfectly captured the essence of original thought.

To wit, original thought is the spark of boundless conviction, the combustible energy from within, and what we refer to as the *magic* behind all creativity, art and—if we really wish to dive deeper—the root of all human expression. Some hidden inner force within compels us to do what is necessary. There is no other option. Noble ideas cannot and will not and shall not be contained—nor constrained. They must be shared. To have meaning, our convictions must connect with others. Burning passion and romance are congenitally linked, yet always require each other for sustenance.

I was reminded of this repeatedly while turning the evocative pages of *Why the Fuck Not?* for the first time.

In the following part-rant, part-treatise, part-plea activist David Litvin bakes us a full multi-layer cake and then he let's us eat it too. His first non-fiction book is a philosophical-political-social-economic mass maze and salvage yard teaming with hidden treasures beneath the piles of external confusion, a smoldering alphabet soup of letters and cleverly crafted words and ideas, a heartfelt and painstaking summation of his own countless hours, days, weeks, months, and years spent thinking deeply about the most serious subjects facing us, our world, and a myriad of universal problems and travesties—the vast majority of these troubles man-made and (if we listen and learn--and act appropriately in time) . . . potentially solvable.

But the clock is ticking. More like, alarm bells are ringing.

In this 21st century, we must seriously ponder the question of our own fate and the destiny of our descendants—will we make it to the 22nd century, and beyond? The odds don't look good.

Our looming doom and peril demands an honest look at the current facts: Global modernization and interconnected social media were supposed to make us collectively wiser; but lies, disinformation, and confusion are worsening. This has spawned an unprecedented confluence of crises.

Throughout the world, dangerous demagogues are worshiped. Superstitions proliferate. Science is ridiculed. Experts are debunked. Journalists are mocked. Ignorance is celebrated. Democracy is in danger. Wars are raging. Half the world goes to bed hungry at night. The other half are likely to die from diseases because they're too fat. Corporations strangle economies. Consumers are enslaved to self-destructive habits.

Personal debt is at an all-time high. Government deficits are out of control. Banks are going bust. Crime is rampant. Another worldwide pandemic could divide us, and even destroy us. We could be just one biological catastrophe or a maniac possessing a nuclear weapon away from a dystopian disaster. Oh, and the world is about to become a giant pizza oven if we don't do something quick about man-made global warming.

Other than that, everything's great.

Early on, David Litvin writes, "This book is based on a very simple premise. The world possesses the resources to feed, clothe, house, and educate every single human on the planet. The truth of this premise is irrefutable and would be affirmed by every scientist and expert on the subject in the world." Just when we need an expression of hope, here it is. Indeed, we can (and should) apply this same positive message and boundless optimism to many of our other man-made problems, as well. Hence, yes, yes, yes, there is *something* we can do—things we can all do and practice—that can make things better and improve our quality of living.

I humbly ask, what is more important than that?

Whether we choose to read—is up to us. Whether we choose to listen—is up to us. Whether we choose to act—is up to us. Whether we choose to share and convince others to join in a global march toward self-preservation and greater happiness—is up to us. It's all up to us. Entirely.

With his characteristic selflessness, wit, passion, humor, and an occasional bit of shock value to keep us all on our toes while pondering the most serious issues we must confront, David Litvin has given us both a manifesto and a toolkit.

David Litvin says what he feels and feels what he says. Let us ponder his words and ideas and add our voices to this greater global chorus of acting on good faith for the universal good.

Nolan Dalla
Writer / Citizen Activist
Thanksgiving Night, 2023

PART I

1

———

INTRODUCTION

People have been declaring the end of the world for as long as there have been people. So far, at least, they have been wrong. That's not to say that mankind has not been victim to an untold number of disasters. We have. Some of them natural disasters, such as plague, volcanic eruptions, famine, and severe weather in many forms. That's just for starters.

Then there are those "plagues" that we have unleashed upon ourselves. War, genocide, country music, nuclear disasters, and social media. Just to name a few. Despite the prediction of gloom and doom, we are still here. But it feels a little different this time, at least to me. In this book we're going to cover a number of things that are converging in such a way that the doomsayers might just be right this time. The threats we face are not like the threats of the past. We have always had our political wars and battles both inter- and intra-national. Just like always. Political turmoil is natural and dangerous but pales in comparison to broader, more basic threats to our survival. Not just as a nation, but as a species.

We now face genuine existential threats to the human

species. Some completely man made. Some influenced by the behavior of man. And still others that seem as basic as the planet simply shrugging us off like some kind of nuisance. Trying to regain its own balance. Its own ecosystem.

We are a fly evading the planetary swatter. At least for the moment.

Honestly, it might already be too late, our epitaph as a species written but never to be read.

But despite what you have just read, this is ultimately a work of optimism. It is my position that we have the opportunity not just to survive but to thrive in ways never before possible and barely conceived.

This is a work of nonfiction that implies truth. But that only goes so far. I have read plenty of nonfiction that contained only the tiniest and tasteless morsels of truth.

With that said, here is my mea culpa. I am biased. My bias will always be to favor reality and survival. And when I say survival, I mean the survival of my country, the United States of America—the greatest country in the history of the world—the greatest experiment in human liberty and prosperity the world has ever known.

But she is in danger. And part of my bias is to do what little I can to save her, to keep the fire burning that was born of the words, revolutionary when written, that all men are created equal. And, if possible, to expand and buttress freedom itself so that it applies to everyone.

I have but one more bias to confess. I am biased in favor of my species. I favor our survival as a species and also the planet that serves as our host.

I performed extensive research in preparation for this manuscript. I have made every effort to be balanced in my approach. All the more when my research led me away from my own preconceived notions.

Our species has never stood on the brink of extinction as we do today. So I will make no apologies for a bias to that which is **real.** A square is a square, no matter how many may call it a circle.

2

THINGS YOU NEED TO KNOW

IF YOU DON'T ALREADY (AND DON'T BE A DICK)

This book is based on a very simple premise: The world possesses the resources to feed, clothe, house, and educate every single human on the planet. The truth of this premise is irrefutable and would be affirmed by every scientist and expert on the subject in the world. What's more, it will remain true, even as the inevitable effects of climate change become more severe and commonplace. Not to be depressing, but we have crossed that threshold as well. Climate change is completely inevitable. We can do everything right from this point forward (which we won't) and there will still be dramatic events related to climate change. If we do better as a species, we can some-what mitigate the effects, but most of all the shitty stuff is going to happen anyway.

The reason you don't see this in the news, even the news not owned by Rupret Murdoch is because it's just too fucken depressing and there's not much we can do about it anyway. By the way I know that fat-ass Rupret is Rupert Murdoch and not Rupret. Rupret was the mentally challenged character Steve Martin played in the movie *Dirty Rotten Scoundrels*. I just got a little juvenile hit of dopamine by calling that fat piece of shit Rupret.

But no, you will never see the headline "We're Fucked," even on legitimate news outlets, because it's just too depressing and might even make us less likely to put up a fight. If the truth were widely understood, our collective response might well be to throw up our hands and say, "fuck it." Everybody goes out and buys a Hummer and we start strip mining for coal in Yellowstone National Park.

I'm getting way off topic here, but there are actually a bunch of things like that. The scientific community knows it. There's not a bunch of conspiratorial cover-ups. It's just not emphasized. For example, sperm counts and fertility rates are dropping precipitously all around the world. There is a halfway decent chance that we are on our way to extinction as a species. This is completely true and has actually been reported quite a bit. But in a matter-of-fact way, without dramatic music and constant repetition, so nobody gives a shit.

OK, just one more before we get back to work. Antibiotics. They are not so much, how can I put this, *working* anymore. We have overused them to the point where the effectiveness of antibiotics is dropping radically and quickly. It doesn't help that our delightful factory farm corporations dump 160,000 tons— yes, tons—of antibiotics into the feed of factory farmed animals every year in the U.S. alone. We are literally stuffed full of antibiotics, even if we don't personally take them and even if we don't eat meat, because the runoff goes into the water supply. I'm guessing you probably drink water, or liquid of some sort, so nobody can avoid this, and scientists are predicting at some point a post-antibiotic world, meaning the really tiny bugs eventually wear us down and win the battle. That would be bad. No surgery would be possible, and you could die from a paper cut. So yeah, that might be bad. But let's get back to the good-ish news. The world can feed, clothe, house, and educate everyone if we want to.

You don't believe me? Look, this book will cover a very wide range of things you may or may not already understand. Before I started working on it, there were a lot more things that I didn't understand. But there is another ridiculously simple premise that underlies everything else: **DON'T BE A DICK.** Those four simple words describe a principle so basic that it can replace millions of words written in thousands of self-help books. Denying or refuting reality is dickishness of the highest order. So, if you refute this basic premise, then you probably are a dick. And this book, and probably air, are not for you. You are a moron, and it is not my job to fix you. Yes, yes, the earth is flat. The moon landing was fake, and Bill Gates put a microchip in your penis once he found it. People like that wouldn't be reading something like this anyway. They are probably on a pilgrimage to the grave site of drug addict and child molester Rush Limbaugh.

OK, hopefully the woefully stupid are gone and we can proceed with those that at least have a clue. There is no exact agreement about when this became true. But any number of factors converged somewhere around two to three decades ago.

But the truth is now, and into almost any conceivable future, we have the ability to take care of every person on Earth. There doesn't have to be anyone homeless. There doesn't have to be anyone hungry. There is no reason for anyone sick to go uncared for. There is no reason to leave anyone uneducated. There is no reason to waste anyone's potential by failing to give them as much education as they can absorb.

All of it is a choice that the world has made collectively and continues to make every single day.

Again, I ask you to think about it. We can feed, clothe, house, care for, and educate *everyone*. But we choose *not* to do so. If I asked you to flip a switch and make it so, would you? If not, then why not? I'm not going to start cursing you out for being selfish or stupid. I am genuinely interested. Part of human nature, thank god, is the ability to feel empathy for others, yet many of us suppress that, including myself on occasion. Since you aren't here and probably don't actually exist, I'm going to try to find the reasons that you, me, and the world have not yet made the choice to provide everyone with food, shelter, clothing, healthcare, and education.

So again, I ask, if you could flip a switch and immediately create a world where every person is guaranteed those four basic things, would you flip that switch? Before you answer, let's add another factor. Consider that if you flipped that switch it would *not* be at the expense of anyone else. In other words, **nobody** would be caused to have a lower standard of living if we made the choice to feed, clothe, house, and educate everyone. In fact, it is much more likely that living standards would rise for everyone. Why that is true is complex and multifaceted, but true nonetheless. We can get into those nuts and bolts later. But there would be no robbing Peter to pay Paul.

Another question: What percentage of people do you think would refuse? How many people would say no? And among those people, what would be their reason? Of course, I would flip that switch. And if you are reading this now, you probably would too. But I believe there are about five percent of people who would say no. Obviously that is just a guess, and your guess would probably be just as good as my own. Imagine if we took a poll of every person on Earth. The people who say no, their no vote is a vote to guarantee that some children will be homeless and/or starve to death. So you would have to have some very strong feelings in order to cast such a vote.

Another question: If ninety-five percent or more of us would vote to flip that switch, why hasn't it happened yet? Why isn't every human on Earth clothed, fed, housed, and educated? All logistical issues aside, it can only mean that the tiny percentage that would refuse wield enormous political and social power. We might be quick to say that the only people who would say no are already extremely rich and powerful. And they would say no out of the fear of losing that power over others. Or fear that their own wealth and social stature would be reduced. Again my guess is no better than yours. But I believe that a fair chunk of the naysayers would be among the poor and powerless. I think it's fair, while also quite childish, to call those people simps. But they are fucken simps. And I believe, without the slightest proof, that they are motivated by self-loathing.

3

———

HOW WE GOT INTO THIS MESS

The reason I believe this is because I have observed that, in every political election in my lifetime, people have voted for leaders they know will spend tax dollars to subsidize the rich and powerful at the expense of the poor and powerless. No one person or group of people could possibly be that fucken stupid for that long. If you voted for Eisenhower in 1952, you got NASA, the interstate highway system, and the Civil Rights Act of 1957, which was the first step in the direction of civil rights. The interstate highway system is arguably the best use of tax dollars by any nation in the history of the world. It produced literally trillions of dollars in productivity gains and continues to this day. NASA took humanity to the moon. Eisenhower was far from perfect. He said as much himself. But I believe he was the very essence of underrated, underappreciated, and underestimated. He stood squarely in the crosshairs of history, and he knew it. His farewell speech in 1961 was one not only of a true and great patriot but with an almost clairvoyant view of the future. The excerpts below demonstrate his understanding of the world as he knew it and the new world of dangers we would face, including and especially the scourge of corruption:

Our military organization today bears little relation to that known by any of my predecessors in peace time, or indeed by the fighting men of World War II or Korea.

Until the latest of our world conflicts, the United States had no armaments industry. American makers of plowshares could, with time and as required, make swords as well. But now we can no longer risk emergency improvisation of national defense; we have been compelled to create a permanent armaments industry of vast proportions. Added to this, three and a half million men and women are directly engaged in the defense establishment. We annually spend on military security more than the net income of all United State corporations.

This conjunction of an immense military establishment and a large arms industry is new in the American experience. The total influence-economic, political, even spiritual-is felt in every city, every state house, every office of the federal government. We recognize the imperative need for this development. Yet we must not fail to comprehend its grave implications. Our toil, resources and livelihood are all involved; so is the very structure of our society.

In the councils of government, we must guard against the acquisition of unwarranted influence, whether sought or unsought, by the military-industrial complex. The potential for the disastrous rise of misplaced power exists and will persist.

We must never let the weight of this combination endanger our liberties or democratic processes. We should take nothing for granted only an alert and knowledgeable citizenry can compel the proper meshing of the huge industrial and military machinery of defense with our peaceful methods and goals, so that security and liberty may prosper together. The power of money is ever present and is gravely to be regarded ...

We pray that peoples of all faiths, all races, all nations, may have their great human needs satisfied; that those now denied opportunity shall come to enjoy it to the full; that all who yearn for freedom may experience its spiritual blessings; that those who have freedom will understand, also, its heavy responsibilities; that all who are insensitive to the needs of others will learn charity; that the scourges of poverty, disease and ignorance will be made to disappear from the earth, and that, in the goodness of time, all peoples will come to live together in a peace guaranteed by the binding force of mutual respect and love.

Please forgive me. I know that was a long and probably boring stretch. I hope you hung on long enough to get his point. Corruption is the greatest enemy we face. Remember that this man was a Republican president. The last of his breed. Can any of you reading this imagine any modern Republican uttering such words? There would be no room for Eisenhower in today's Republican Party. He could foresee the potential for corruption far beyond what was possible in his time. Yet as visionary as he was, I can't believe that he could have imagined what his own party would become. Because if you voted for Ronald Reagan in 1980 and 1984, you, an ordinary citizen, got less than nothing. Resources were diverted to even more military spending and tax cuts for the wealthy. Organized labor was decimated. He began the destruction of America's miraculous middle class that accelerated and resulted in the largest stratification of wealth in human history. The banks that funded Reagan's campaigns were rewarded with elimination of regulations that resulted in the so-called S+L Crises in the early nineties that ended up with the hapless Bush the First paying off the problem with taxpayer dollars. Fun non-fact about the Bushes: Did you know that they aren't allowed to wear wrist watches because it makes an unpleasant jingling noise in the pockets of Saudi Arabians?

The plain fact is that these banks stole about $1 trillion by lending to each other and then defaulting on the loans. It really was as simple as that. It cost every American alive in 1992 $3,000 each. Bottom line: The banks paid Reagan to steal a trillion dollars. And there is more, so much more. It would take a whole set of books to fully explore how much damage that one man did to the world. I can't help it though. I have to give you just one more. He gave Nicaraguan drug cartels free rein to flood black neighborhoods with crack cocaine, then imprisoned millions of blacks in prisons owned by another set of corporate donors to his party and campaigns.

Part of that campaign was just a touch of outright treason by Reagan. Anybody remember Ollie North and the Iran-Contra Scandal? This is a hundred percent true and extensively documented. Reagan sold arms to Iran and used the proceeds to fund the Nicaraguan Contras who were fighting against the legitimate Sandinista government. This despite a law passed by Congress that explicitly forbade military or financial support for the Contras.

That's bad enough. And here's where the lovable, but fat, repulsive, and evil Rupret Murdoch comes in. This part is almost certainly true, but I cannot claim that it has been definitively and legally proven. An Australian national, Murdoch was already a media mogul and had numerous meetings with Reagan and his handlers during the early eighties. Murdoch was a public cheerleader for Reagan and assisted Reagan with a massive propaganda campaign on his various media outlets. The idea being to demonize the Sandinistas, promote the Contras, and help distract attention from the arms for hostages deal that Reagan made with Iran during the runup to his victory over Jimmy Carter in 1980. The deal was that they hold on to the hostages long enough for Reagan to win the election, which they did, and then release them as soon as Reagan took office, which they also did. Treason. There is no other word that applies. For his assistance in manipulating the public, fat-ass Rupret got U.S. citizenship and the ability to legally buy out and corrupt a fuck ton of previously legitimate news organizations, including *The Wall Street Journal.* Can I prove this part in a court of law? No. Is there a shred of doubt that it actually happened? Also no.

By the way, Rupret got to eat yet another cream pie from Reagan. In 1986, Reagan repealed the fairness doctrine. This was the FCC regulation that broadcasters must present both sides of political issues. Simply put. The repeal of the fairness doctrine paved the way for the likes of Fox News and Rush Limbaugh to make a mockery of fairness and provide imbeciles with a 24/7 diet of divisive, false, racist, and nonsensical propaganda. The whole subject is depressing and enough to make me not give a fuck if we fill ourselves nose high with microplastics and sail off into extinction. But suffice to say, if this were the *only* horrible thing that Ronny and his corporate bosses did, it would still be enough to make him far and away the worst president ever inflicted on Americans. Including Cunto "Grab them by the pussy" boy.

And there are a couple more pieces to the media puzzle that help us to understand how we have arrived at corruption central. There were no true glory days of the media to harken back to. For close to two centuries, the news media was newspapers and nothing else. And they were hardly neutral and incorruptible. Neither Joseph Pulitzer nor William Randolph Hearst were saints. The overall shittiness of news reporting in the current era is more of a historical norm than an outlier. But there were some small slices of integrity from time to time, most importantly during the dawn of the television era in the 1950s and 1960s. And shards of that greatness still remain if you look for them.

In those times, the network news divisions were not expected to make a profit and created the phenomenon of the "trusted news anchor." If you are anywhere around my age, you just immediately thought of the great Walter Cronkite. If you are a little older, you may have thought of Edward R. Murrow. If you are younger, you might think of Tom Brokaw or Diane Sawyer. Let's be honest—probably all of us just thought of Will Ferrell and Ron Burgundy.

But those times evaporated with the consolidation and corporate ownership of almost every news outlet. Also evaporated were the restrictions on just how much media one entity can own. Worse yet, the internet destroyed the economic foundations of newspapers in ways from which we have still not recovered, leaving them hollowed out shells to be easily preyed upon by hedge funds and billionaires for their own gain. Almost everything you see now is from a news aggregator and not a reporter. We have yet to figure out an economic model that makes ethical and impartial reporting possible. Social media is designed to show us exactly what we want to see to keep us engaged and watching, pulling us deeper and deeper into the rabbit hole. And the nonstop lying we are exposed to is not an accident. It's a tactic. A profitable and incredibly dangerous one. It has deprived us of any objective reality on which to base a conversation or negotiation. It leaves us lost, lonely and angry. And an angry person is the easiest to manipulate for profit. Just ask Steve Bannon.

So can you grasp the ease with which corruption takes root? Do you get the picture here? It's a very simple triangle. You give money to a politician. He makes the rules that allow you to steal and plunder. You give part of the proceeds back to politicians to keep the scam going forever. After all, it's cheaper and easier for corporations to make the law rather than break it. Once you understand this absurdly simple corruption, you will find it everywhere, in virtually everything. It is at the heart of almost every problem we have as a society. I am tempted to make a connection between the **Triangle Trade of Corruption** and the Triangle Trade of Slavery. I'm not going to make the case that the modern triangle of corruption is the moral equivalent of the slave trade, but our corruption now is so massive, so pervasive, and so effective that it has turned giant swaths of the population into economic slaves. Let's face it, there is no justice without economic justice. There is no freedom without economic freedom. Unless you want to count it as the freedom to starve. This is a HUGE part of the reason that we, collectively, have chosen NOT to feed, clothe, house, and educate everyone. Look, I'm getting tired of saying feed, clothe, house, and educate. For the rest of this rant, I will refer to it collectively as the **Big 4.**

And just for the hell of it, I'm going to name the quest for the Big 4 as a political movement, even though it doesn't exist yet. Now If you're going to have a genuine and durable political movement, you are going to need a catchy name, phrase, or title. Actually, I don't know if that's true. The Emancipation Proclamation was pretty crucial but doesn't exactly roll off the tongue. So maybe it doesn't need to be catchy, but I am going to go for that anyway. It can't hurt.

Ladies, gentlemen, and everybody those two words don't cover—oh yeah, and kids too—I present to you the political movement that could actually save our lives and our species. I present to you 4 For All.

4 FOR ALL

I don't mind telling you that I think it's perfect.

But before I hurt myself with all the patting myself on the back, let's define our terms. When we're talking about the **Big 4,** what we really mean is a Large 7:

- **HEALTHCARE**
- **ENERGY**

- **HOUSING**
- **FOOD**
- **WATER**
- **CLOTHING**
- **EDUCATION**

Those are the fundamental components. Assuring those seven basic things for everyone gives us a chance to continue as a species, as well as a level playing field on which to live and work.

I don't consider accomplishing this goal to be the *end* of anything (except perhaps unnecessary suffering). Rather it is a chance for us, human beings, to *begin* to unlock our real potential as a species. It would mark the true **beginning** of civilization. A relatively clean start and a truly level playing field. It is about more than things. It is about setting a baseline of human dignity. Since we now have the means, we have the moral obligation to set that baseline, that minimum dignity that each of us deserve without exception. Even Flat Earthers, Tucker Carlson, Rupert Murdoch, The Brothers Koch, and people who think *Friends* was as good as *Seinfeld*. Yes. Everyone.

This is not a matter of capitalism, Marxism, communism, socialism, or any other "-ism." We will place a granite floor at the feet of humanity. That ground level of granite is that we are ALL assured of the fundamentals of existence on which one can build a life. When I envision this new world, I see it as utopia of human freedom and dignity based on a **real** version of free market capitalism and democracy. Not the current explicitly corrupt version. What we now call capitalism is a corruption-riddled corporate oligarchy. As you will see as we go along, what we are living through now is almost the exact opposite of true free market capitalism. It is a perverse, reverse form of capitalism where the consolidation of wealth and power makes a mockery of democracy. **4 For**

All is not the enemy of capitalism and democracy. It is its savior.

Along the way, we are going to discuss all seven components of the **Big 4**. And I am not naïve. I understand that there are a million-plus things standing in our way and a lot of things are going to need to go very right if we are to have any chance of building that floor and regaining and assuring our personal and collective dignity. But isn't it worth a shot? Stay with me. Keep reading this book, even when I resort to being a sarcastic asshole. Because more than anything else, it is a cry for **dignity**. For myself and everyone. We all deserve at least that much.

For the purposes of this book, we will break it down to four and categorize them in this manner. We're going to clump food, water, and clothing together. We're going to put housing and energy together. So that leaves us with a **Big 4** that looks like this:

- Housing/energy
- Healthcare
- Education (as much as we can stuff into you)
- Food, water, clothing

That is your Big 4.

It's easy to say and understand yet stands for something that would be utterly transformational for everyone residing on this planet through no wish of their own. **No wish of their own?** Again, something so basic that we don't ever stop to think about it and are not even sure how to ask the right questions. But I'm willing to take a wild shot at it.

Do you know anybody who *asked* to be born? Did you or anybody you know ever request this assignment? We are all literally **visitors** to this planet, this existence. We are summoned into presence and consciousness. To my knowledge, not a single one of us made a reservation at this Hotel

Earth. Comparing Earth to temporary lodging is not fair . . . to hotels. Because if Earth were a hotel, it would be worse than the most roach-infested shit hole you ever got stuck in. Yet here you are. Were you somewhere before? Are you going somewhere after? Did you have consciousness before conception that you just can't remember during your stay here at Hotel Earth? Will you have a conscious existence after your visit? I don't know, but I can't see why not. Seriously, what is the point of plopping down a bunch of sentient beings in this shit hole? Just to have us spend our time literally running, working, slaving, and begging for our lives? It makes me think this must be part of something bigger. But who the fuck knows? Not you. Not me. And certainly not Joel Osteen or your drug dealer.

OK. There are the questions. I don't know what the fuck to do with them. We are born. Some of us wander around for eighty some odd years, and then we all check out sooner or later. Again, to where? Who knows. There's no shortage of preachers and salesmen who will make up answers to these questions if you feel strongly enough about demanding answers. They will take your money and tell you that you are a piece of shit that needs to suck some savior's dick to avoid damnation. In the case of the Catholic Church, that last sentence was way more literal than any of us should be comfortable with. The Catholic Church is a repulsive monstrosity. Let's face it. It attracts sick people who prey on the most helpless in the most horrible of ways.

But religion itself in the abstract is just as insidious and destructive. Why? Because virtually every religion teaches two wildly destructive things to children too young to do anything but believe it, and they have no choice but to make it part of who they are, and with inevitable and heartbreaking consequences. First, they teach you that you are born bad. Children are defenseless. When you tell them they are bad, they will believe you. The second is they teach you that your natural sexual desires are evil. Again, we are too young to do anything but believe it, so we come out of the starting gate feeling that we are "bad" and can only be saved by limitless devotion to an invisible savior. One thing every savior has in common: They need your money.

We have been programmed to believe our natural sexual urges are evil. You can't make sexual instinct go away by suppressing it, feeling guilty about it, or feeling like a piece of shit for having it. Because religion doesn't just tell you that you and your sexual urges are evil, they also prevent you from finding healthy ways to channel those instincts. They then manifest themselves in other, far less healthy ways. The result is legions of fucked up people. From flashers to child molesters to pedophile priests, to the entire Republican Party. All of it can be traced back to their healthy sexual urges being repressed and the ever-present self-loathing it creates.

We have all these unanswered questions and people who do tremendous harm while pretending to answer them. We have seen that they do tremendous harm in exploiting our need to think we know. I would be remiss if I didn't explore some of the other horrors these fucks made up in their quest to steal a few bucks and treat women like property.

Most religious texts use this pretext of a god to inflict shittiness. The most common is misogyny. The sheep fuckers who wrote most of this garbage couldn't satisfy a real woman with a box of dildos. They, like most men, naturally questioned their own desirability to women and their feelings of inadequacy. Probably with good reason, but no matter. These fears are so central to the male psyche that virtually every religious text struggles mightily to subjugate women as a core tenant. The damage inflicted by this nonsense is incalculable. Men have been programmed to believe they are "better" than women, but men still subconsciously know better. Women have been programmed to believe, if only subconsciously, that they are "less" than men. It was Eve who ate that literal *god damn* apple.

This is much like black people have been programmed to believe that they are less than white people. And I am sorry to say that they believe it too. Again, if only at the subconscious level. This harm has been created, magnified, and made part of who we all are for more than a millennia. It's going to be tough to shake. But shake it we must. Even the luckiest and smartest among us have to spend our whole lives trying to pull the horrible weeds out of our brains by the roots. The evil that was planted in their brains (still remains, said Paul Simon) from the moment they were born. The idea that we are born bad and our sexual instincts are evil. It's there. In all of us. Because it was planted in us before we had any ability to do anything but believe it. Before we had any ability to defend ourselves with critical thinking. Before we move on, I want to point out something in an unusually large and descriptive font. Something that is one hundred percent true. Something that should be obvious to everyone by now but isn't. Or at least they can't admit it. Not even to themselves.

4

———

RELIGION IS CHILD ABUSE

You know it. I know it. And the fact that there's still a whole bunch of religious douchebags out there doesn't change this actual objective truth. This is something we will get into a little later: objective reality and the fact that a square is a square, even if ten trillion people believe it to be a circle. I am not denying that point of view, opinion, and perception matter. They matter a lot. But **objective reality remains**. And she is a persistent bitch. Earth is round. Lots of people deny that and they are free to do so. I don't want to have lunch with them, but they have every right to a stupid opinion, to a point, because if we try to do things based on assuming Earth is flat, there would be tragic, although probably quite humorous, consequences.

I understand calling religion child abuse is a serious accusation. So let me define it a little better. *Religious teaching of anyone under the age of eighteen is child abuse*. I am prepared to defend that statement. As we discussed earlier, children, especially small ones, will accept as truth that which they are told by adults, especially subconsciously. We have already established that one of the basic precepts of all our popular religions is that we are born bad and broken in one form or another. A child is told that they are a sinner and are broken and that their natural sexual drives are evil and sinful. If you were to remove religious "popularity" and prevalence and teach those things to children, there would be a world full of outraged parents. Even more, imagine those things taught out of religious context altogether. Would that not be considered child abuse by almost everybody? One last way of looking at it. Imagine a swap. Any swap you want. An Islamic teacher teaching Islamic doctrine at a Christian school. Now flip those. A Christian teacher teaching Christian doctrine in an Islamic school. In both of those scenarios, I believe the parents would believe their children have been abused. And they would be right. Only their own brand of horseshit is palatable. "Don't you dare abuse my children. That's my job. Well, my God's." So the bottom line is:

RELIGION IS CHILD ABUSE.

Before we move on, I want you to grab a flashlight and shove it in whatever hole gives you the best look around your own brain. Now try to honestly ask yourself, who would you be if you had **not** been taught that you were born bad and that your sexual urges are dirty and evil? Take as much time as you need. Get as much help as you can because you're going to need it. If you are genuinely able to be completely honest with yourself, this project will take quite a while. Same thing with a **4 For All** world. It's a slippery fucker. If you take the concept seriously, it's nearly impossible to grasp all the implications. To sort out all the tendrils. Trust me, I'm still trying myself. I've been trying for years and I'm still trying. This book itself is part of me trying.

Now let's get back to whatever it was that we were doing. Oh yeah . . .

With all these questions that have no real answers, there is one thing we can all be relatively certain about. None of us asked to be here. Nobody logged on to any celestial *Expedia* and booked a stay at *Hotel Earth*.

In all of this built in uncertainty, there are a couple of things you can be sure of:

- Everyone requires the **Big 4**.
- No one is fully able to provide the **Big 4** for themselves. We all need help.
- Almost every one of us is taught that we are sinners and must struggle for and **earn** all the basics of continued existence.

We are all born naked, helpless yet mentally constructed to want to stay as long as possible. Again, all of this through no fault or decision of our own. So are we all entitled to a living, aka the **Big 4**? Fuck yes!

It's as if you invited—no, not invited—**forced** your neighbor to come over for lunch. But when she gets to your house, you tell her to go out and farm for a sandwich. Fuck no. You brought her here, now feed her. Same thing with all of us. We are guests of this planet through no choice of our own. Every single one of us deserves full and complete sustenance and support with absolutely no strings attached.

Can you fit that concept through your skull? Can we fit that concept through our skulls? It goes against everything we've ever been taught. Every one of our teachers and law books and religions and economic theories tells us that we are not deserving. We suck. We must work. We must struggle. We must sing for our supper.

But it's not true. All of us deserve everything. Every soul deserves the **Big 4** at the very least. For most of our history that simply wasn't possible. We weren't capable. But now we are. We *can* do it. We *must* do it. Let me repeat that: Now that we **can** do it, we **must** do it. **It is the <u>only</u> moral imperative that matters.** Now that the world is capable of feeding, clothing, housing, and educating everyone, we must **DO IT**. It is truly the very least we can do for our guests.

Here's the part where that little, tiny part of your brain kicks in and says, "Wait a minute! All this shit has to come from somewhere. We can only give things to people that come *from* someone else." That feels right, doesn't it? It's been beaten into us so completely that it feels completely natural to think, "Someone gets, someone gave. Somebody gained, somebody lost." That feels so right, so natural, so real.

Except it's all bullshit. And that bullshit has an actual name. It's called a *zero-sum game*. A zero-sum game presupposes that there is a hard cap on everything, and someone can only gain something by someone else's loss. There are a dozen donuts in the box, and if you eat one there is one less for me. It doesn't really work that way, so try to forget that stupid shit. No, really, forget that stupid shit. In reality, there are nearly infinite donuts. We can always fry more donuts than even the fattest fucks can eat. But it's not so easy, is it? Search your soul. Throw a couple of C batteries in the flashlight again and take a good look around. It's in there. That feeling that if someone wins, someone must lose. If someone got, someone gave. OK, now admit it to yourself. Admit that you have been programmed to believe it and then, please, throw it away. Piss on it, wait for it to dry, then set it on fire and scatter the ashes because <u>it isn't real.</u>

There is enough of everything for everyone without anyone losing anything. We can have **4 For All** and nobody would lose so much as a paper clip or a dick pic.

So there we have it, a political and economic movement for everyone, everywhere, **for** everyone everywhere. Like any good revolution it needs a proper battle cry. For instance, during the American Revolution our brave fighting men would shout,

"God, fuck the king." That didn't really happen. But it was fun for a moment to think so. I was picturing these guys with pointy hats and muskets marching in formation and singing "God, fuck the king."

5

IF NOT, WHY NOT?

Now back to the people who would say no that aren't billionaires. What do you suppose their reasoning could be? What could compel a not-rich person to vote against the **Big 4**? Maybe this: <u>**There are people who don't deserve it.**</u>

And when those poor people make that decision. It's their own laziness and sloth they are sure of. What they are really saying is *I don't deserve it. And nobody else does either.* It's the exact same reasoning that keeps them voting for people who will fuck them and people like them. So let's work this out together. What makes people hate themselves enough to believe that no one, especially them, *deserves* anything? I'm having trouble describing this and grasping at straws because on the surface it makes no sense. The stuff we talked about above, the deeply held belief that we are bad and sinful, has fingerprints all over this shit. It's why we have trouble believing that anyone deserves anything. No one will ever admit to believing that anyone deserves something for nothing. I'm not even sure that any of us actually believe that anyone deserves anything for nothing. How many times have you heard older people talking about younger people and saying, "They think the world owes them something." That is arguably one of the worst things you can say about someone. But let's examine this for a moment. It represents something so basic that we barely notice it.

As we talked about above, we really do believe that all of us must sing for our supper in some form or another. Then it follows that nobody really believes that anyone deserves anything as a basic given. Everything in the world is transactional and part of that bullshit *Zero-Sum Game* philosophy. Somehow, we give a pass for royalty and people who are born rich, which these days might as well be the same thing. What is it in us that demands that everyone must **earn** everything except for the people lucky enough to come sliding out of a lucky vagina? Perhaps, and this is just a guess, but perhaps it's the corollary to the concept that we all need some "other" to be better than. Maybe the reverse is true as well. Maybe we need someone to be "worse" than. Maybe we need "royalty" or the economic or criminal equivalent. We give them a complete hall pass. We just accept that they are rich and secure and always will be. We revere them. We build them up into royalty, into Kennedys and Bushes, bootleggers, and traitorous cunts. We are OK with the fact that not one of them will ever have to lift a finger against their will.

Hero worship? Living vicariously? Something to aspire to? But there is something that makes us perfectly fine with laziness, but only from the rich and powerful, while the starving children born into hopeless circumstances are expected to somehow lift themselves up by their own bootstraps. But I can assure you, these poor bastards have no access to bootstraps, whatever the hell those are.

These concepts, so basic to our being that we barely notice, have to change. And they can change. In the same manner as we resist and change other instincts. We don't shoot everyone who annoys us. We usually don't beat up the guy who lets his dog shit on our lawn. We don't kill the guy riding by on a motorcycle so loud that it causes everyone around him actual physical pain. (In this case, maybe we probably should.) The point is that even the most entrenched patterns, even the most instinctual thoughts, can change—and sometimes very quickly.

Tangent alert: When I was young, you could smoke everywhere. My father owned a beauty salon and had three cigarettes lit pretty much all the time as he would run around the floor of his business, smoking each one. People smoked everywhere. Consider this: I myself smoked on airplanes. Something that is almost inconceivable today is something almost everyone used to do. The truth is, an airplane is little more than a ball of pressurized air and incredibly flammable jet fuel. It is, in essence, a flying bomb, hurtling through the air at thirty-five thousand feet. And there I sat, happily smoking away with most of the rest of the passengers. You could smoke in the hospital around compressed oxygen. You could smoke, as Robert Blake did on *Johnny Carson's Tonight Show*, seventeen cigarettes at once.

A generation later, you can only smoke in your room, with the lights off, under a blanket in a room hermetically sealed by a group of certified transgender gynecologists. That was a really fun phrase to say and it's also a bit of an exaggeration but doesn't change the point. Our society went from smoking freely everywhere to barely smoking at all in an incredibly short time. We can do it. It's all the more impressive when you consider that you had massive, powerful tobacco companies fighting for every inch of ground. But finally, the Marlboro Man climbed down off his horse and died of lung cancer. The original "Marlboro Man" actor, Wayne McLaren, died of lung cancer in 1992 at the age of fifty-one. So yes, we can do this.

Maybe there are some people that, for one reason or another, are so disgusting that we have no wish to help them. Maybe drug addicts, Miami Dolphins fans, and lazy people are so repulsive that you, and part of us all, would just as soon see them suffer and be denied even basic necessities. It's a form of "they got it coming." It's true. There are a vast number of dimwitted, stupid, and more or less worthless people in the world. If I were to deny feeling that way myself, I would be utterly disingenuous. I don't do disingenuous. Shitty people will always be with us. Does that mean they don't deserve to be people?

If your concern is that we will become a bunch of fat lazy fucks, don't worry, we already are. One thing has been consistent since the start of the Industrial Revolution: Fewer and fewer of us are needed to perform any real work to produce the goods and services we all need to ensure the **Big 4** for everybody. At every turn, new technologies have replaced the need for human work. The car put all the horse and buggy drivers out of work. The riding crop industry took a pretty radical downturn. This phenomenon has happened over and over and over in almost every industry. With each new innovation, the experts predicted that technology would take over every human job, leaving us poor, downtrodden, and out of work. It never really played out that way, but it is beginning to happen now. This time for real. Computer and wireless technology replaced millions of jobs but replaced a fair number of them with other jobs. AI technology will replace untold numbers of high-paying jobs. The plain truth is that less than ten percent of us need to work in order to produce the goods and services that assure the availability of the **Big 4** to the entire world population.

We have the ability to create heaven on earth. The only thing stopping us is us. We have a choice.

"CHOICE" in this context means a fuck ton of different things. I'm not delusional. Politics, ignorance, nationalism, racism, misogyny—especially racism and misogyny—and plain old human nature stand in the way. And probably always will. But that changes nothing. Poverty, homelessness, hunger, desperation, and despair continue because WE WANT THEM TO. But WHY?

A particularly troublesome part of the human condition is the need to be "better" than others. Our egos require that we constantly compare ourselves with one another. I think we are all familiar with the phrase "keeping up with the Joneses." Our collective need to compete is built into us at the molecular level and is an inescapable result of evolution. (If you have a problem with evolution, please see above. Fuck you and go away and continue to go away until further notice.) Those of us alive are the descendants of the winners of an all-out war for resources that has been continually fought for thousands, if not hundreds of thousands, of years. It is then no surprise that greed, envy, and ruthlessness are built into our genome.

And by the way, it's OK. We have the ability to overcome these instincts if we choose to. Not unlike a dog who can be trained to fight his instinct and not eat the food right off your plate sometimes. These inborn traits manifest themselves in so many different ways that I don't even want to bother with a depressing list of examples to prove the point. So I'm going to go with just one quote and one thought experiment.

President Lyndon B. Johnson once said, "If you can convince the lowest white man he's better than the best colored man, he won't notice you're picking his pocket. Hell, give him somebody to look down on, and he'll empty his pockets for you."

This is pretty self-explanatory and completely true, like a lot of things Johnson said. Humans suffer. That is an undeniable basic part of life. But we feel better knowing that there are always people even worse off than we are. It's a really repulsive part of our collective personalities. But tough shit, it's part of what makes us us. We can "act" better than that. We can rise above some of our ugly instincts, but it takes effort, way more than most of us are willing or able to give. You can teach your dog to stop eating your shoes, but it will still be her instinct to eat them. Especially your favorite and most expensive ones. Vast scientific research continues into why dogs always eat your favorite shoes instead of that shitty pair that never quite fit right. It's a mystery almost as important as the disappearance of every pen you ever had and the odd single sock that always remains in the dryer.

Now for the thought experiment: A 1952 Topps Mickey Mantle baseball card recently sold at auction for $12.6 million. Why is it worth that much to someone? The short and correct answer is because it is rare. Maybe there are only one or two, or a handful, but certainly not enough to go around. So it's fair to say its value is based on its rarity. "Rarity," by definition, means few, and that more people want it than can possibly have it. So the thought experiment is this: What did this person buy for $12.6 million? Yes, he got a small piece of old paper with the face, name, and stats of *Mickey Mantle*. What makes it valuable is that YOU can't have one. No one but a very small number of people can have one. Exclusivity is the point. In this case, exclusivity cost $12.6 million. I could argue that the entire collectible industry is based on the principle of "Fuck you, I have one, you don't, *na-na na-na na-na*."

Does the person derive $12.6 million worth of pleasure from looking at a small piece of paper made seventy years ago. No, I think the pleasure comes from knowing that only he can have one. I could produce fifty billion of those Mickey Mantle cards and give a few to everybody. They wouldn't be seventy years old, but they would produce the exact same sensory experience. I could even make the fucken things smell like bubblegum. But no one would pay $12.6 million for them. So I argue that the value is based solely on the competitive nature of exclusivity. Only that one person can have that one particular piece of paper, regardless of how easily millions more could be produced. Yuck, it's kind of gross when you think of it that way. It's only valuable because YOU can't have one. But it's the truth.

But we now live in a world advanced enough that there is enough for every man, woman, and child to have all the essentials of life without exception. Hell, we could give everyone a handful of 1952 Topps Mickey Mantle baseball cards.

Why the fuck not?

6

____

NOW

Before we get into the why not, let's figure out what that would mean. There are some questions in the world that are so big that we aren't even sure how to ask them. But I'm going to give it a shot.

What would it mean if everyone were assured, from the moment of birth, that they would always have food to eat, a roof over their head, clothes to wear, and as much education as they can absorb to realize their fullest potential?

Because I feel like it, I'm going to start this section off with a quote by a character from the *Star Trek* spin-off series *Deep Space 9*. He is a member of an ultra-capitalist species known as the Ferengi. If you were to shake hands with one of them, it would be best to count your fingers on the way back. But it's a pretty complex series and he is a very well-realized character by the end of 167 episodes. Quark ends up being a pretty good guy. For you non-Trek fans still with us, in the *Star Trek* universe, humanity has more than achieved **4 For All**. He had this to say about humanity:

Let me tell you something about Hew-mons, Nephew. They're a wonderful, friendly people, as long as their bellies are full and their holosuites are working. But take away their creature comforts, deprive them of food, sleep, sonic showers, put their lives in jeopardy over an extended period of time and those same friendly, intelligent, wonderful people will become as nasty and as violent as the most bloodthirsty Klingon. You don't believe me? Look at those faces. Look in their eyes.

Again, for you non-Trek folks, the Klingons are a brutish, warrior species. And he is right, is he not? We ARE a friendly bunch when our bellies are full. And we do have the tendency to be completely amoral shit stains when we are hungry, cold, or otherwise deprived of the basic comforts of life. The direction I'm going with this is an important one. How much of our shitty behavior would evaporate in a world of universal **Big 4**?

Again, because I feel like it, I'm going to present a thought experiment that fits, but only in the largest possible sense. As I write these words, twelve people have died in mass shootings in two separate incidents **this week.** There have been 144 mass shootings in the United States so far this year resulting in more than seven hundred deaths and five hundred serious injuries. Oh, and by the way, as I write this it is **April.**

How does this relate to anything we're talking about? In a **Big 4** world, how many guns would Americans own? For reference, right now we possess 1.2 guns per person. In other words, there are more guns in the United States than there are people. Just for the record, we are talking about civilian gun ownership and not including any branch of the military. Not even the national guard, which is what the Second Amendment *actually* authorizes to have guns.

The Second Amendment guarantees the right of a well-regulated militia to bear arms, which in modern terms would specifically mean each state's National Guard. Not Earl Jimmy

Joe Bob Ray Jimmy. Don't believe me? Well, first of all, FUCK YOU. Then, fuck your sister. Then, fuck your sister's sister. I would say fuck your dog, but I like dogs. It's you I don't like. Besides, you probably already are fucking your sister if she's too fat, slow, and diabetic to get away. You and all the other dickless twats that want a gun because they just aren't anywhere near man enough to live without one. I get that you don't agree with me. But you know who does? Every Supreme Court from the eighteenth century up to 2008. What changed in 2008? you may ask. Or you might not ask. No matter, I will answer anyway.

To know what happened in 2008, you first have to know what happened in 1971. That was the year humanity got the Powell Memorandum stuffed up its ass. It's still in there. Stuck in humanity's ass. Causing all the problems that an individual person might have with something horrible stuck in their ass. That was a fun paragraph to write. I got to say "ass" a lot and make light of something truly terrible. But the Powell Memorandum was anything but fun. If you are alive today and reading this book, there is a pretty good chance that Lewis Powell personally made your life a good bit worse than it would have been if some other sperm had won the race to the awaiting egg in his mother's hole. The half century of corporate fuckery that he unleashed might well have been avoided. The corporate overlords that now rule your life may very well have been kept at bay.

First, you have to remember that this was a time that consumer advocates like Ralph Nader were in the process of forcing the American auto industry to adopt seatbelts. A relatively new technology that had actually been donated to the world without any attempt to profit from it, by the Swedes of the Volvo Corporation. Because they knew it would save lives. They are saints. Could you imagine any company now making such a decision? Fuck-fucken-fuckity-fuck-fuck NO! Into that era of expanding consumer and environmental protection came Lewis Powell with the Memorandum of Death. The memo itself became nothing short of a blueprint for the corporate takeover of the world that **has** come to fruition. To this day, I would like to think it would have changed his thinking if he could have known how much wealth and power would be concentrated in so few hands. Just as our Founding Fathers could not have known. But this we can never know.

Before we start digging up our boy Powell, let's have a little chat about the Founding Fathers. I have read about and studied these men my whole life. What they pulled off in creating this country and our constitution was spectacular and nothing short of a miracle.

But they weren't gods, and they certainly weren't perfect. If they had been perfect, there would not have been another century of slavery. But they were damn good and way ahead of their time. With that said, what do you suppose is the "point" of the Constitution? I can hear the word "freedom" coming back from you and, yes, the Constitution was in large part about defining and guaranteeing a set of personal liberties. Good stuff. Groundbreaking, great stuff. But it was way more. These men came from a kingdom. And at that time, there were kingdoms all around the world. A king commands absolute power —all of the power.

I would argue that, more than anything else, the Constitution was about one thing, and that's fragmentation. It was a high wire act of trying to disperse and fragment power as much as possible. In defining the three pillars of their shiny new federal government came the separation of powers of the executive, legislative, and judicial branches. What's more, it defined that powers not explicitly granted to the federal government would remain the purview of each state within these newly founded United States.

Why am I boring you with this history shit? Good question.

The point of everything they were doing was to prevent power from being consolidated in any one person or institution. It was an amazing balancing act of fragmenting power and assuring freedom. And the damn thing worked, and it still works despite recent and ongoing efforts of that tubby orange fellow.

Yet there is something within human nature that seems to yearn for a king. I've been wrestling with this concept for the last few days and have arrived at a conclusion that is quite dismaying: Human beings seem to be wired to want some kind of all-powerful force. I'm no psychologist, but it doesn't take one to know that we must have some type of innate need for a strongman or some kind of imperial power.

Something about our collective makeup wants power to be consolidated, whether it be in an institution, a person, or a god. Royalty is an example of both. Drug cartels are an example of both, right? You had the cartel as an imperial power and a Pablo Escobar to be the face of it. Maybe it's as simple as a compelling need to have something outside ourselves to aim our emotions at and to blame our problems on. A large and powerful *them* to worship, fear, respect, honor, and die for. It's a way of transferring responsibility for our own condition.

A certain amount of power consolidation is a good thing and it produces order. As much as we might complain about it, and as imperfect as it is, we are all pretty glad to have the U.S. government, an army, and some police to call on the neighbors for playing loud country music. Without some degree of power consolidation, there would be chaos. Chaos in politics, at our jobs, from our drug dealer, our businesses, and our princes. But there is one small problem.

Power has gravity. Power attracts more power. Having power enables something to gain more and more power. It's as natural a phenomenon as gravity itself. Like a snowball rolling downhill, ever bigger and faster. Too much power consolidation turned people into Nazis and have turned lots of other people into virtual Nazis.

It's as if we need to reduce and categorize things neatly in order to think or talk about them. If I were to say the words "civil rights movement," what would be the first thing to pop into your head? Was it Martin Luther King, Jr.? It was for me. And I bet it was for a lot of you as well. Why? Because he's a big deal and involved millions of thoughts and actions by millions of people. MLK was a civil rights leader and certainly a great man. But he was one person among many. Logically, we all know that he didn't create the civil rights movement by pulling a rabbit out of a hat, but we pull the entire thing together in our minds and put him on top of it. It's like taking a shortcut.

That's the best I can do in trying to describe our collective need to consolidate power. To have a single person or entity to look up to, to cower before, to fear, to worship.

Why is this more of a problem today than ever before? Technology. It is communication and travel that enables consolidation of power in ways that were not possible before. In 1776, what made a person rich? There were really only two things you could own that would matter: land and people. Technology and travel have made it possible for individuals and entities to be millions of times richer and more powerful than the richest people on Earth in 1776. Money equals power, more directly than ever before. The power of money pushed aside the very rules that were supposed to keep them at least somewhat separated. The massive consolidation of power and money **has already destroyed democracy**. If you can't see that, I will not curse at you and call you a fucken moron. I will do worse. I will simply pity you.

With that, we come full circle back to the Founding Fathers. Their express goal was to prevent the consolidation of **political power**. They did virtually nothing to prevent the consolidation of money and power and its eventual subversion of democracy and political power. Why? Because as brilliant as these guys were, they were not prophets or fortune tellers. They couldn't see into the future. In their day, you could only own so much land, so many people. They couldn't conceive of a world where a multi-trillion-dollar corporation could be run from a broom closet in Delaware. There was no way they could have known how much money and power could be consolidated into so few hands and how the power of money could overwhelm and dominate politics. Homework assignment: Google "regulatory capture." That explains almost everything.

Had they known, they would have done something about it —I would bet my dick on it. Just like they designed the Constitution to disperse and fragment political power, these smart men would have found a way to disperse and fragment the power of money. "All men are created equal" would require a sequel, a way to fragment and disperse **economic power** in the same way that they were able to do with **political power**. If they had only known. But they couldn't and they didn't. And now we are left with a steaming pile of dog shit that is the remains of our democracy. And it's even worse than that. The money that rules us is not even *American* in any meaningful sense. The U.S. is a wholly owned subsidiary of Exxon, ATT, Apple, and a few dozen other largely foreign-owned corporations that control almost all of the resources. All of the **Big 4**.

The Founding Fathers created the Constitution to enshrine for all time that all men are created equal. They were awesome within the limits of their time. But in the current day, there can be no equality without some type of economic equality. I'm no commie. We can keep free market capitalism at the heart of any system that does for economic equality what the U.S. Constitution and the Declaration of Independence did for political equality. Let's call it *The Equal Sequel* to the Constitution. And it will include everyone, not just "men." But it sure as shit won't be easy.

So back to Powell. Remember him? His memo was basically a call to arms for business to stop playing defense and start fighting back politically against the Ralph Naders of the world and the people fighting to label tobacco as an unsafe product. He was even against seatbelt mandates. He was hideously, horribly wrong, but not dishonestly so. In fact, Needle-Dick Nixon made him a Supreme Court Justice and he went on to achieve a modest record of distinction in that role. He even joined the majority on the landmark *Roe v. Wade* decision that legalized abortion nationwide. The right that women are now losing to the racist white Christian nationalists, corporate power, and the general Republican self-hatred of themselves and their maniacal desire to exert control over women that they are certain they could never satisfy with their withered, pathetically small schlongs.

There was no way this man could have known in 1971 just how much power and influence technology would permit these companies to acquire. And remember another very important thing before you order a Lewis Powell dartboard—is there such a thing?—in his time, the companies he was defending were American corporations. There was a very popular saying of the time that encompassed the conservative view of America: "What's good for GM is good for America." I don't agree with it, but it retains some measure of validity. The point was that, when American companies do well, American people do well. I get it. I don't agree with it, but I get it. What he did not foresee, nor could he possibly foresee, was that in the current age there would be **NO SUCH THING AS AMERICAN COMPANIES.** The companies that strangle humanity are primarily foreign owned. At the very least, with very powerful foreign influence. Now combine that with the declared singular purpose of every company on this particular fairly attractive planet, enhanced shareholder value.

7

ENHANCE SHAREHOLDER VALUE

Because of that, they do not—and CANNOT—give a shit about you, your job, your wellbeing, your roads, your electrical grids, your bridges, your food supply, the safety of your food supply, your safety at home or work, or anything else that matters to the wellbeing of this country and its citizens. **THEY CANNOT AND DO NOT CARE.**

The absolute only thing that can produce any meaningful change, the only thing that would give us any chance of stemming the tide of complete and total corporate oligarchy, would be to make fundamental changes to the concepts that make a corporation a corporation. It would be simple to do yet almost impossible to actually achieve. Simply change the phrase that defines their purpose. Right now, **EVERY** corporation charter contains the same phrase, the same singular goal no matter what business they happen to be in: **ENHANCE SHARE-HOLDER VALUE.** Under that premise, they can, do, and **must** act as amoral animals that cause death, dismay, pain, environmental catastrophe, and a list of horrors that would fill another series of snarky books. But the fix is almost as incredibly simple as it is nearly impossible to perform.

Change every corporate charter to include the following:

Enhancing shareholder value is our first priority, but not at the expense of other reasonable priorities. These other priorities include but are not limited to:

- **The wellbeing of all affected by our behavior.**
- **Our employees, the communities that we serve and wish to serve.**
- **The environment, the earth, and the wellbeing of all who reside here.**
- **We will make no attempt to evade reasonable taxation.**
- **We will make no attempt to affect political change unless it serves the needs of our corporate stakeholders, which include employees, the communities we serve, the environment, the earth, and our shareholders.**

As you can see, that would be quite a change. And you, like me, have trouble envisioning it coming to pass. But it would go a long way toward creating a *Star Trek*-like heaven on earth. But the funny thing is that, even without being part of the corporate charter itself, most companies used to behave at least somewhat ethically. Their behavior was not that of a remorseless sociopath that corporate behavior has evolved into today. That even meant making some decisions that would not necessarily advance the interests of shareholders at the expense of the larger good. That philosophy, and corporate behavior, changed when the economist Milton Friedman (a close associate of Mr. Powell both personally and intellectually) emphasized that a corporation was duty bound to act **only** in the interest of shareholders.

Ronald Reagan was among the first to embrace the douchey *shareholders only* philosophy, and it has since become the very heart of Republican politics. I'd be willing to bet quite a bit that these nudniks barely understand its meaning or impact. But it's the perfect philosophy to create the **Triangle Trade of Corruption** that we talked about earlier. To refresh your memory, let's go with another example.

Home internet in the United States lags well behind most other developed nations and is also quite a bit more expensive. The reason is yet another perfect example of the **Triangle Trade of Corruption**. More than ninety-five percent of homes in the U.S. have no more than two choices for home internet service. Some forty percent have but one option. The two major players are AT&T and Comcast, and they basically control an ATM. They have no incentive to improve service and can charge basically whatever they wish. And, of course, they hang up on you when you call to complain that your bill was an extra $50 for no apparent reason. They pay off the government to make sure no one else can disrupt their duopoly. Technically it's called *barriers to entry*. At least that's what an economist would call it. But what it really means is that both companies control government officials to maintain those *barriers to entry* to make absolutely certain that they face no meaningful competition. **It is the exact opposite of free market capitalism.** It is, again, very simple very effective corruption that harms virtually every one of us. The result? Both companies treat their customers/hostages like shit because they know they can. Where are you going to go? They basically trade five percent of market share a year back and forth between them. They abuse, hang up on, overbill, and finger fuck their hostages to death. Each year, a few of their victims switch from one turd to the other and—surprise!—we still get covered in shit.

Here's a slightly different version of reverse, perverse capitalism. Do you have car insurance? Don't answer, I already know you do. Why? Because it is required **by law** in every state except New Hampshire. And even there, if you choose not to insure, you must post a bond and prove you have the money to pay if you hurt someone or something with your car. So the result is that this is an insurance product you **must** buy under penalty of law. That doesn't sound like a *free market* to me. Unless the threat of prison somehow translates to *free*. Yet the suppliers of auto insurance are free to do as they please. In most places, they can charge whatever they please, base their rates on whatever they please, and basically jam massive, multi-colored dildos directly into our financial asses however they please. Someone please explain to me how this is free market capitalism. You have a guaranteed, legally bound, captive pool of customers. And an industry that can do whatever the fuck it wants. No wonder Warren Buffet bought Geico and that fucken lizard.

Here's a radical concept, since we all **must** purchase the product if we drive: How about if we pay for it through gas taxes or something that places the fair expense and burden on the people who need it without including corporations who make billions off a captive set of customers? Maybe we could use those billions to do stupid things like fix roads and bridges and build highways. A free market is only a free market when both parties have a choice. When they don't have a choice, we have another word for it: extortion. In this case, government mandated, government sponsored extortion. Hmm . . . why would we allow that? Maybe it's the millions in campaign contributions that the insurers give to the politicians. Yes, my friends, yet again, the **Triangle Trade of Corruption.**

Depending on where you live, you probably have exactly one choice of company for electric power. Here in Florida, it's FPL—Florida Power and Light. They can charge whatever they want because you have no choice but to pay them whatever they want, or you can sit in the dark heat. They pay off whoever they need to in government to maintain their monopoly and to charge whatever they wish (again google "regulatory capture").

They even use the money they extort from us to make and air these lavish commercials that tell us exactly how wonderful they are. Again, a simple triangle. Pay off the government, make a fuck-ton of money, kick some back to the government to keep the scam going. I don't know exactly what the fuck you might call this, but it most definitely is not capitalism. And it's definitely not a free market. It is corporate oligarchy and corruption, and it's choking us out. But I do genuinely love capitalism —we should try it some time.

Sometimes corruption is so simple. It's the equivalent of passing a law that says everyone has to send this company a check. When you look at electric utilities, auto insurance, and internet it really does feel that way. It is the force of government. Do you *have* to buy auto insurance? No, but you do if you want to drive without getting ticketed or arrested. Do you *have* to buy electric power? No. But if you want lighting or air conditioning (in Florida), you need to pony up whatever they tell you to. Do you *have* to have internet? No. But aside from entertainment, you need those services to find a job or a dozen other things that enable you to participate in the economy. Most job applications are solely online these days. The truth is you are completely coerced to do business with them. Usually by law.

So you should be asking yourself, and quite reasonably so, what the fuck does any of this have to do with guns?

8

GUNS, AND THE BIRTH OF MODERN CORRUPTION?

And, once we are done with the gun shit, what does that have to do with the **Big 4**?

Glad you asked. The NRA were among the first to take Powell's ideas and turn them into a murderous nightmarish reality. So let's take a little dark, horrifying journey with the NRA.

The NRA began its life as a sportsman group. They were dedicated to safety, training, and recreation as part of a sporting life. For most of their existence, they were in favor of most restrictions on guns, particularly handguns.

Tangent alert: I'm against any form of hunting and not even slightly less so if you plan on eating what you kill. The reason I'm even against hunting for food is a bit convoluted. If I go to McDonald's and choose to eat what they call a hamburger, I know that the animals involved were factory farmed and existed only for the purpose of being eaten. In other words, they never had a life to lose. They were conjured into existence for the sole purpose of being eaten. Now that is horrendous, and I could subject you to a couple more books about how incredibly horrible factory farming is for any number of reasons. It's incredibly harmful to the environment, it's causing antibiotic resistance as we saw earlier, and it subjects the animals to incredibly cruelty. When you hunt in the wild for your own food, you are taking the life from an animal that *has* an actual life and would otherwise have lived out its life naturally. So, to me, it's actually worse than factory farms. In that respect at least.

I simply can't get on board with killing something unless it's specifically threatening my life or those around me. Specifically going out with the express purpose of killing things that have caused you no harm is undoubtedly mental illness. You don't think so? Killing other than for self-protection is OK? Just killing something that is defenseless and harmless for no reason is not mental illness? If you believe that, then you are fucken nuts. It's another case of people ignoring and avoiding the obvious because a large group of people have chosen to believe the same nonsense. To call the square a circle. The square is still square no matter how many times people call it a circle. It's still square, no matter how many times *Fox Nuuz* calls it a circle. Reality persists, so stay away from sharp objects and make sure to read the instructions on a box of toothpicks. And try to remember to remove the fork from your mouth before you chew. Or don't. I really don't care. You're an idiot.

Just like religion, the only reason it's not considered mental illness is that there are a ton of people who believe the same crazy, stupid shit. But that changes nothing. Killing something for sport is morally wrong and a sure sign of mental illness by any form of objective measure. A person who would do that is sick. Now for the non-fact part. I believe it again springs from the painful fragility of the male ego and their desire to prove manliness. They have unusually small genitals and are convinced that they must kill animals and dominate women physically in order to reinforce their manhood. Scientific evidence? Nah! True? Probably. For both religion and killing for no reason. Let's not forget that the primary purpose of religion is to subjugate women.

Let's get back to the NRA. From 1871 until the 1970s, the NRA was what I described earlier: a group of men, armed with mostly rifles and shotguns, playing with their cocks and balls and out for a good time in the wilderness. This all changed when a fine man named Harlan Carter took over the organization after a period of upheaval called *The Cincinnati Revolution* at the NRA convention in 1977. Fun true fact: 1977 was also the year that *Harlan Carter* was accused, tried, and eventually acquitted of murder. It was, as far as I could tell, an O.J. kind of thing. Everyone knew he did it, but "oh well," it was a white guy shooting some brown folks and that just wasn't particularly frowned upon. He quickly moved the NRA from Colorado to the D.C. area and turned it into a full-time lobbying organization with the vast majority of funds coming from gun manufacturers themselves. Very quickly it went from a sportsman club to a lobbying juggernaut.

These days, they wield so much political power that just the hint the NRA might help your opponent is enough to keep politicians in line. Just the threat is usually enough. They don't even have to spend a dime. In the old days, the sporting fellas were in favor of almost all gun regulations. Under Harlan Carter and right up to this minute, they are against any and all regulation of guns. As I said before, most of their money comes from the gun manufacturers. Some of it comes from the Second Amendment yahoos. And there is pretty good evidence—not quite enough for me to declare it as fact—that strongly suggests that foreign governments, especially Russia, cozy up to the NRA and give them tons of money with the express purpose of sowing divisiveness and making sure that a fuck ton of kids get mowed down in classrooms. There isn't much that screws up a country more than the constant fear of burying your children.

OK, so let's talk about how we got here. Since the eighteenth century, the Supreme Court has had numerous opportunities to find an individual right to bear arms amid dozens of cases brought before the court. But they never found any such right until 2008 because it doesn't exist. It's abundantly clear to any objective person that the Second Amendment was meant as a way for the newly formed federal government to assure the individual states that they would continue to be able to arm and defend themselves. This was a big deal at that time because many states were concerned and afraid of a national army that could impose their will on any state. The Second Amendment was their way of assuring the states that they would not be at the mercy of a federal government that would be the only ones with arms. To be fair, it should also be noted that there is no part of federal law that specifically outlaws guns. But no, the Second Amendment does not even remotely guarantee the right of an individual to bear arms. Again, I could write a couple more books and still not cover all the reasons that the yahoo redneck no-dicks are wrong.

But I can't help it. Here's one of my favorites. I hear all the time in person and on social media about all the countries that lost their freedom because their governments took guns away from their citizens. There are so many reasons that this is so fucken stupid that it makes my head spin. But for expediency, I'm going to focus on one thing: Many gun owners and, of course, our friend *Rupret* over at *Fox Nuuz* say that we need guns to defend ourselves from some lefty, commie-elected government out of control.

Here's the thing, I could recruit every gun owner in the United States—let's put them all in the same place—and each of them can aim their little pee-pees—correction, their *guns*— at a single U.S. military aircraft. For the hell of it, let's say a run-of-the-mill, not-exactly-cutting-edge F-16 Fighting Falcon. The United States Government would win that confrontation with a single almost obsolete fighter jet against three hundred million dipshit gun owners. The point: Armed private citizens would have exactly no chance against any government military that wished to oppress them or, god forbid, let gay people get married or some similar horror.

Just one more, the self-protection argument. Jimmy Earl Joe Bob Jimmy needs a gun for protection because some Mexican might come and try to steal a six pack out of his trailer. The self-protection argument is actually a good one. Very visceral. Everyone, me included, can relate to it. We all want to feel safer. We all want to feel as if we have some control in a world where we have precious little control to begin with. I so get it. I so understand this motivation and instinct that I'm not even going to be a smart-ass about it. But the facts just don't jive with our feelings. The only thing I can really compare it to is that most people feel safer in a car than they do in a passenger jet, even though flying is definitely safer. It's not even close. But driving makes us feel safer because we have "more control."

This was another case where meaningful statistics were difficult to find. Steve Bannon, one-time Senior Counselor to President Trump famously said that the trick to winning public opinion and creating chaos was to "flood the zone with shit." When it comes to finding solid stats about guns being successfully used for self-protection versus various bad outcomes, the zone is most definitely flooded with shit. So let's define what we're talking about. If an individual legally owns a gun, what kind of comparisons can we make about potential outcomes. On one hand, you could potentially use that weapon to protect yourself or others from someone trying to commit a violent crime. On the other, you or a family member could be harmed by the gun by way of accident or suicide. There is also the possibility of the weapon being stolen and used for criminal and/or violent purposes.

It's an issue that is so emotional, on both sides, that finding the facts is like trying to end a conversation with an insurance salesman. Sorry, I promised not to be a smart ass. Eventually I found a very broad statistical consensus. It's kind of wide but very real. If you live in a household with a firearm, it is between five and eleven times more likely that you or a family member will be injured or killed by that weapon than it is that the weapon will be used to fend off an intruder or prevent a crime. Just like the driving-versus-flying conundrum. Owning a gun makes us **feel** safer but actually places us in considerably **more** danger. That is the truth.

So how did the Supreme Court suddenly, after 175 years, "find" an individual right to bear arms in the case known as *Columbia v. Heller*? Well, it came straight out of the Powell Memorandum playbook. It was a multi-pronged attack that involved the NRA, the gun industry, and paid-off plants in the world of legal academia. The whole shit show played out over a couple of decades as some legal experts were paid to publish specific things in legal journals that would allow the bought and paid for justices to gin up some legal pretext that did not exist. But never mind all that, just read the fucken thing:

"A well-regulated Militia, being necessary to the security of a free State, the right of the people to keep and bear Arms, shall not be infringed."

You would have to be a fourth grader to read this for anything other than what it means. Well, either a fourth grader or an amoral fuckface industry that wants to sell every single fucken gun possible and doesn't give a shit about stacking up the bloody bodies of dead children.

It took them four decades, but it worked. They created a "right" that doesn't exist. And lots and lots of Americans are dying, but that's just fine. Ruger doesn't feel a thing. Neither Smith nor Wesson has lost a single moment of sleep over the dead kids. The body parts. Or the fear. How about the fear? How about the fear that every American parent feels in their gut when they send their kid to school not quite knowing if they will ever see them in one piece again? But the story has a happy ending. The gun manufacturers make a shit ton of money, and the Russians get to poison our democracy. See, all better.

Here is even more about this already unbelievably evil shit. You, me, and every other American taxpayer gets to pay for it. Here is a really interesting economics term called *externalities*. If just this single economic concept was widely understood by voters, this world would already be a much better place. The fact that it isn't is another very long story that would require several volumes. But suffice to say that it has to do with the desire to pray to Jesus in school and keeping those uppity black kids somewhere else. Because I feel like it, I will add one more detail: Republicans have been in an all-out war to destroy public schools since the *Engel v. Vitale* decision that removed organized prayer from school.

Ruger sells Jimmy Joe Bob Ray Ray Bobby Jim Joe Cunt-Face Weak-Ass Piece-of-Shit Jimmy Joe Ray Tommy Fuckface Shit-for-Brains Bob a gun at Wal-Mart. Private transaction, right? That's our boy capitalism and all that. Ruger and Wal-Mart sell the weapon and Fuckface cashes his welfare check and buys it. That's it. Just the three of them involved, right? Wrong! There's that little issue of externalities.

You see, the rest of us are affected by that private transaction in a whole bunch of ways. It's kind of the same principal as why it's illegal to sell crystal meth. We don't collectively give a fuck if someone tweaks themselves into the grave. But we, as a society, have decided that the *externalities* of buying and selling meth are just too much for the taxpayer to bear. So we make it illegal. With booze, we price in the externalities of selling alcohol, which are incredibly expensive. Lost productivity, drunk driving, deaths, hospital costs, funerals, courts, police patrol for drunk drivers, etc. The externalities, meaning the external costs to taxpayers of a private transaction are massive. A guy walks into a 7-Eleven and buys a twelve-pack—a private transaction. But the costs to the taxpayers are massive. So what do we do? We tax the living shit out of it. And that's exactly **what we are supposed to do** in a functioning free market capitalist democratic country. In fact, managing externalities is one of the most important roles of a government within a free market capitalist democracy. It is specifically meant to protect taxpayers from the costs imposed on them by private transactions. You want to drink? Great! You are free to do so. Just don't ask the rest of us to pay the cost.

But when it comes to guns. Not only did they successfully invent a right that didn't exist for 175 years of prior jurisprudence but they are also forcing every taxpayer to pay the externalities. Even if you have never pulled a trigger, you not only get to bury your children, but you also get to pay for the privilege. You pay taxes so that Wal-Mart can make a fortune selling guns. Jimmy Bob can feel just a little better about his tiny pee-pee, the NRA gets to go play golf with Putin, and YOU get to pay for it all. Now I would call that some pretty darn effective lobbying. Oh yeah, I would call it evil. A word I don't throw around all that often.

While we're on the subject of externalities, let me introduce you to some other stupid stuff that you, our loyal taxpayer, get to pay for to the benefit of the foreign investors that own the corporations who own your elected officials. I'm not even going to bring up alcohol and tobacco because we do reclaim most of their externalities through taxes. But here it is anyway, a quick word about the numbers I'm using. I consulted at least seven or eight different sources to find estimates and averaged them out to get what I hope is the closest and fairest numbers. They will be in the ballpark, if not right on home plate.

- **Tobacco** – $180 billion annually

- **Alcohol** – $250 billion annually and I suspect that one is low.

Now the ones you personally pay for:

- **Guns** – $280 billion in taxpayer money a year, and that's almost certainly low.
- **Fast Food** – $150 billion taxpayer a year, and that number is **extremely** conservative. Their Big Mac, your tax dollars.
- **Bottled Water** – Ready for this? Jesus, this one needs a drum roll . . . Here you go—you get to pay **$2.2 TRILLION** a year.

Now, in all fairness, that last point is inclusive of plastic in general because I couldn't find decent numbers with just single-use water bottles jizzed out. But while we are on the subject of jizz, remember when we talked a bit earlier about how our fertility rates are dropping a lot and that we may very well be on our way to extinction as a species? Yeah, that little thing. Well, it turns out that it's the chemicals from the water bottles that are one of the suspects, if not **the** prime suspect. A study published in the journal *Human Reproduction Update* in 2018 found that exposure to phthalates and BPA (the shit that's in the water bottles) was associated with lower sperm counts, decreased sperm motility, and increased sperm DNA damage. OK, lower sperm counts I already knew about, but *decreased sperm motility*? Holy shit! So not only are there fewer swimmers, but the little bastards are slower too. Now that's what I call proper externalities. Not only does it cost me $2.2 trillion a year, but it also slows my swimmers? To be honest, if I knew better at the time, I would've actually taught mine to swim backward. But hey, hindsight and all.

And while technically not exactly an externality. We should

consider the costs of taxpayers subsidizing employers who quite literally pay their employees a starvation wage. I say literally because one study found that almost ninety percent of Wal-Mart employees qualify for SNAP, which we commonly call food stamps. Similar results were found throughout the fast-food and retail industries.

So you might as well shop at Wal-Mart and eat at McDonald's because you're paying their employees whether you like it or not and whether you go there or not. You, the taxpayer, are pretty generous with Amazon's employees too.

Does this make any sense to you? Is this actually capitalism in any way? Let's be blunt. They pay their employees dog shit, so little that they can't afford to survive without public assistance, so we subsidize their employees while they make billions in profits. It is exactly as if the taxpayer is handing money directly to these companies' bottom lines. They make billions, we pay their employees. That's not capitalism. That's not free market. That is corruption, plain and simple. Or more directly, corporate welfare.

Billion- and sometimes trillion-dollar companies transfer their costs on to us, and they make the profits. Two quick stats before we get past this repulsive subject. Numerous studies have found that the average low-wage worker receives between $5 and $8 an hour in public assistance. They have also found that, for every Wal-Mart store, their employees receive about $2 million a year in public benefits.

You're going to find this type of thing all over this book. It seems that what passes for capitalism in the twenty-first century is actually more about this. Giant, mostly foreign-owned companies figuring out a way to pass what should be their own hard costs on to the taxpayer and into their own pockets.

I **don't** mind my tax dollars going to help the needy, handicapped, or unemployed. I **do** mind my tax dollars going to subsidize the pay of working people. Either their employer should pay them or their employer should not exist. This is the very definition of *corporate welfare.* If your business plan requires the taxpayer to subsidize the pay of your employees, then you don't have a business plan—you have a way to swindle taxpayers to your own benefit.

Oh, and that $2.2 trillion from plastics is child's play compared to the biggest and greatest externality of them all. It will get its own section, with a fully attempted but sure-to-fall-short explanation of the world of corruption that surrounds us and keeps it front and center in our lives. How's that for a tease to keep you reading?

OK, enough of that. Let's get back to **4 For All.**

PART II

9

WHAT WOULD IT MEAN TO LIVE IN A BIG 4 WORLD?

WHAT WOULD GUARANTEED UNIVERSAL 4 FOR ALL MEAN? AND IN WHAT WAYS WOULD THE WORLD BE DIFFERENT?

I have said repeatedly that there are numerous questions that are so massive that we can't even properly ask the question, let alone find an answer. In this case, I think we have defined the question pretty well. But the answers are a whole other thing. The question has so many different and far-flung implications. I would guess that the answers touch on elements of every social science. A partial list includes:

- Anthropology
- Civics
- Criminology
- Demography
- Economics
- Education
- Environmental studies
- Folkloristics
- Gender studies
- Geography
- History
- Industrial relations

- International relations
- Law
- Library science
- Linguistics
- Media studies
- Communication studies
- Political science
- Psychology
- Public administration
- Statistics
- Sociology
- Social work
- Sustainable development
- Public relations

There are philosophers who have called the United States "the great loneliness." I think the meaning is that our focus on individuality and personal achievement is unique but has the negative effect of isolating us from each other. You could also make the argument that it is this drive to achieve that has made this country great. And it is very possible that both are true. It's not mutually exclusive and not necessarily a bad thing.

A feature of this duality is expressed in our "needs," both personal and common. Need itself is at the heart of most of our actions and most of our problems. We "need" money to live. This gets us out of bed every morning to fight rush-hour traffic to get to our jobs. We "need" to feed our kids. We "need" to protect our country. Every manner of both good and bad behavior is justified by "need."

Why did my ex-wife steal my Rolex and pawn it? She "needed" to it to feed her habit for drugs and gambling. Her "need" pushed her to do other things as well. She stole $30,000 and, when confronted, blamed the theft **on her own son.**

There is a point to this walk down Memory Lane. NEED IS

THE EXCUSE FOR EVERYTHING. And all of us have a different definition of *want* and *need*. All manner of bad behavior can be justified by need. Everything from Nazi genocides to stolen watches are justified by a perception of need.

So I guess what I'm saying is be careful what you think of as need and try not to mistake it for that which you merely want. If you can keep your needs simple, you can keep your masters few. And have a better chance of mastering yourself.

4 For All is the way for us to manage and reduce *need* in our society. With all our basic needs met, it becomes much harder to justify immoral behavior in the name of need. None of us will *need* to lie, cheat, or steal to feed our families. We will face fewer moral dilemmas that pit need against ethical behavior.

It will not make us perfect human beings. But it will make us *free* human beings. Free of the moral traps that our needs set for us.

One thing I want to babble about briefly is the question of housing.

10

HOUSING

HOUSING, AND WHY RACISM IS STILL THE THING

A major element, maybe the biggest element of the **Big 4**, is housing. A whole lot of housing will need to be constructed to even approach the ideals we have discussed. The issue has proven to be a stubborn beast even among rich nations and, perhaps especially, in rich metropolitan areas within rich nations.

The problem is extremely complex but a pretty big chunk of it can be attributed to a single thing. NIMBY. NIMBY is an acronym for **Not In My Backyard**. Public housing? Not in my backyard. Multi-story building? Not in my backyard? Low-income housing? Not in my backyard? The public is in favor of a whole lot of things that would help. Just as long as it doesn't end up in their neighborhood.

Quick stat: The City of San Francisco has created exactly **one** new dwelling for every **eight** jobs the city's dynamic economy has created over the last two-plus decades. It doesn't take a genius or mathematician to figure out that this makes no fucken sense and is a massive problem. It creates absurd rents and real estate values and turns a terrifying number of people homeless. It's hard to imagine a more "liberal" city than San

Francisco. The problem, as it usually is when it comes to housing, is complex. But a huge factor is a form of NIMBY. San Francisco suffers from the self-inflicted wounds of a massive tangle of regulations in the form of zoning, environmental restrictions, height restrictions, and a surprisingly big one—large zones that prohibit multi-family dwellings in favor of single-family homes. There is also the question of "historical sites and zones." And then there's a significant, loud portion of the population that is simply against development of any kind. Well-meaning laws have made it way too easy for a tiny number of people to tie up and prevent building.

Simply put, mostly well-meaning people doing mostly well-meaning things have made it almost impossible to build enough housing in the United States. Look, no matter your politics, we all can understand that everyone needs a place to live. I think any politician could make a career out of simply saying "build, build, build." Yes, we care about the *green-spotted owl* and the *thick-dicked tiger*, but at the end of the day, every one of us unspotted, thin-dicked humans needs a place to lie down. Just do whatever it takes to keep building housing until it is cheap and abundant.

Housing problems are by no means unique to San Francisco. These effects occur in every major city, and quite a few small ones to at least some significant degree.

The aftermath of the COVID pandemic made a couple pieces of this problem much, much worse. First, the U.S. government printed close to $5 trillion during the pandemic. It then proceeded to hand out all but four percent to the mostly foreigners that own the corporations (the rest of it those little $600 checks you may or may not have gotten). There is evidence that a sizable chunk of that money ended up going to buy up real estate in the United States, which is still considered safe harbor to foreign investors. The other factor was the work-from-home phenomenon. Suddenly many workers found that they didn't have to live in expensive areas anymore to do their job and emigrated further and further from city centers. These two factors, combined with historically low interest rates, led to explosive growth in real estate prices. By the way, it's a bit off topic, but imagine if the government had taken that $5 trillion and spent it on America instead of handing it out to their corporate owners. If they had just sent it to the same people who gotten the $600 checks, it would have been more like $15,000 to $20,000 per person. Imagine the economic jolt from that! Just to put it in perspective, $5 trillion would have paid every college student's tuition, paid for Medicare for all, and repaired every road and bridge in the United States with a bunch left over. Instead, the money went to mostly foreign investors who used it to bid up our real estate and lock most Americans out of the American Dream. Well done! But let's get back to real estate.

Being anti-development is kind of hip and has always been considered something of a liberal purview. But it is in no way limited to people on the left. In fact, being against development is one of very few things that often unites liberals and conservatives. Normally I would celebrate unity. But let's stop and think for a moment about what it means to be anti-development, whether an apartment building in your neighborhood or a massive tract devoted to a whole new subdivision or city.

I think we are far enough along here for you to know that I am at least somewhat of a proper environmentalist. I'm not all about laying waste to forests and animal habitats to build ugly boxes for morons to live in. In general, I think it's a pretty good idea not to destroy the only planet that we have to live on.

But let's take a closer look. When we say we don't want that land cleared and that subdivision built, what are we really saying? In that little, tiny, and very shitty portion of our brain, we're thinking, "I already have a house, why should we build more? Besides, look how cute that owl is." It's kind of like saying, "I don't have any kids, so why am I paying taxes for schools? Why should I pay to build a road that I won't drive on?" It's literally an antisocial, sociopathic line of reasoning. And now that I think about it, it has been at the heart of Republican politics since the Powell Memorandum. Again, grab that trusty flashlight and take a look around inside. Am I right? Is there a little bit of that attitude in you? Of course, there is. You know there is. Not across the board, and certainly not every person in every situation, but it's there. We ALL think that way to some extent sometimes. Whether we admit to ourselves or not.

If you live in a single-family home in the suburbs, what would you do if someone wanted to build ten thousand apartments for low-income families in your neighborhood? Be honest with yourself. Would you really be happy about it? I'll be honest with myself. I wouldn't like it. I would probably be worried about all the same things you are. Will it bring crime? Will it harm my property value? Will there be too much traffic? Will it bring "undesirables" to the neighborhood? That's an interesting one, right? Undesirables. It's OK, let's go there. Who is "undesirable" is different for different people at different times. But let's be honest with ourselves, shall we? In the United States, "undesirable" in this context is virtually interchangeable with "black." Those ten thousand new apartments might bring black people to your suburb. Undesirable. Again, I suck. We suck. "Suck" in this context means that we all have our own set of biases and, yes, probably racism in some form beaten into us. It's not your fault unless you decide to live it and use it as an excuse. I can do better. We can do better. You do, in fact, have to *try* not to suck. It often doesn't come naturally. It's not instinctual. It's not our collective default setting. Not sucking is a choice. Try not to suck.

PERSONAL ANECDOTE ALERT: I'm not sure we can even "own" a house. A few years ago, I was living in a modest 1,500 square foot villa on a nice, but slightly disreputable golf course. I owned it outright. There was no mortgage. Yet when I added it all up, I was paying almost $1,500 a month to live in a house I fully OWNED! And that wasn't even counting water, power, and cable. No, it was just the combination of real estate taxes, homeowners' insurance and HOA fees. $1,500 a month to live in a house I "owned." To me, that means that we never really "own" property. The best we can hope for is to live there. If I failed to pay the taxes or fees or insurance at any time, "my" house can be taken away from me. So how is it even "mine"?

Part of the problem with building enough housing is almost existential. It has to do with its place within our personal financial wellbeing. That is to say, it is the single most important element of both personal and generational wealth. And that will, unfortunately, bring us back around to another familiar issue—racism.

The U.S. government formally created, reinforced, and promoted separation of the races, mostly through Federal Housing Administration policy going back to at least to the New Deal programs of the 1930s. The practice of redlining basically enforced racial segregation and created, and in effect imprisoned, poor, mostly black neighborhoods, proving that racial housing segregation was no accident and still has incredibly harmful effects to this day because generational wealth in the United States is almost always tied to real estate and home ownership.

Blacks were denied these opportunities and still are, at least to some extent. So anyone who says the effects of slavery and racism are in the past are, at best, deluding themselves and are more than likely just full of shit. Anecdotally, the country has millions of homes, sold and financed cheaply to returning white GIs in the years following World War II. Those new homes cost a few thousand dollars and are now worth hundreds of thousands, if not millions. Many became and continue to be the backbone of generational wealth for those families. I don't begrudge them, but we can't ignore that black people were purposefully excluded and did not get to share in that boom, even though it was largely funded with their own tax dollars. Not to mention those black GIs shared in defending this country from an existential threat and were then denied the basic opportunities that their white counterparts enjoyed. It is impossible to overstate how big of a difference this made in generational wealth. It's disgusting and shameful. We can and will do better. The first step is to stop blaming the victims. Stop pretending that the shameful behavior of the past doesn't affect the present.

In calling the housing issue existential, part of what I am trying to help us understand is that housing has developed into something that means more than just a place to hang your hat. It has become a storehouse of wealth to maintain and pass on financial wellbeing. In some ways, it has become something of a casino, with investors large and small buying, flipping, and renting houses to build wealth. Who hasn't seen those ads from people with a "proven plan" to make you rich through real estate. I myself have been a beneficiary of this effect. The home my father commissioned in 1980 for $30,000 will now become the pillar of security for my own retirement. I can't help but wonder how many black families were denied that same opportunity.

But now we have the tools, technology, and resources to build enough housing, even in the poorest and most densely populated areas of the world. It's probably the most complex multifaceted issue of the **Big 4**, but most certainly **not** intractable. One way to close the real estate casino is to just build, build, build to the point where housing is for housing, not for gambling.

This brings us full circle. Remember that $5 trillion we gave away? That would have been way more than enough for the government to have built **forty million** new housing units across the country. There are several ways to do this, but basically the government can build forty million new units and sell them somewhere around a percent or two above cost, then provide the financing for families to acquire them. In the long run, the government is likely to break even on the investment if not actually realize some small gain. In the meantime, there would be plenty of housing and values would moderate nationwide. The casino would be closed and speculation discouraged. Housing would become what it was always supposed to be—a place to live.

Now, let's talk a little almost random shit and try to use our imagination.

11

IMAGINATION

I'm giving you all an assignment. Imagine having been born into a **Big 4** world. You and everyone else know that at the very least you will ALWAYS have food, clothes, shelter, and as much education as you can absorb? That is an absolute concrete floor beneath your feet. **No one can ever be homeless or hungry.**

How long do you think it would take for you to process it reasonably and honestly? Pick a single day and go through that day thinking about what would be different had you been born into a **Big 4** world. I can tell you that, in my case, it has taken literally forever. Every day I find and consider new ways in which my world, and the world overall, would be different. I have thought about it every single day multiple times ever since I first considered it. I don't remember when it first started. But even in my daily life, I am astonished at how different almost everything would be. How many shitty things wouldn't be part of our daily lives?

I was born lucky. If you are reading this book, you, too, were probably born lucky. I was born into a situation where I always had a pretty good chance to avoid poverty without the need to do menial labor. Sure, I had numerous opportunities to fuck it up. A couple of wrong decisions or some bad luck, and it could easily have gone south. It still could.

One of the hardest things for us to do as human beings is put ourselves in someone else's shoes, really trying to see the world through the eyes of someone else. One of my few points of pride in my own life comes from the fact that I have actively cultivated this skill. And it is a skill. I try to understand the view of the person sitting across my desk, in the next car, or screaming his lungs out at a football game. I don't practice this out of a sense of altruism. Let's be grandiose and call it a form of enlightened self-interest. In the big picture, even this is a behavior affected by the need for the **Big 4**. Trying to know and understand the behavior and motivation of others is part of a skill set that helps me to avoid poverty. A particularly useful skill.

There are a lot of invisible people in our lives. Let's put aside those that you never actually see—people like the guy who stands waist deep in chicken guts at a factory farm, the person whose slender Chinese fingers carefully placed your iPhone into its elegant packaging, or the second mate on the oil freighter that was part of the reason there was gas at the 7-Eleven. I won't hazard a guess at how many invisible people are part of your life and toil relentlessly on your behalf. It's reasonable to say it's a four-digit number or more and that almost all of them work much harder than you do for much less than you make.

But let's forget them for the moment and think about the *visible* invisible people who make your life possible. *Visible* invisible? Yes. The guy pushing a broom in the lobby. The woman scrubbing the toilet in the restroom. The people working in the hot, greasy kitchens of every fast-food restaurant. The maintenance guy who changes the lightbulbs and repainted your office. Hell, even the young waitress who took your order at Applebee's, the place you tell yourself you only went because the spinach and artichoke dip was half price after 9 p.m.

I spent most of my adult life in the casino business. A pretty good part of it as a poker dealer and then a long stretch in management. Before I get into this, I want to ask a question that I have never found a simple and satisfying answer to: Why do rich people gamble? First, let's define "rich" in this context. Rich means having enough money that you and your immediate family have enough money to assure the **Big 4** and some luxuries well into the next generation. In contemporary numbers, let's say a net worth of $7 million and up.

Why would someone in this situation want to gamble? What do they have to gain? If they somehow beat the odds and win, they will be what? Richer? If you are already rich, you have nothing to gain that will improve your life and situation. The only thing you can do is lose. Almost everybody loses in a casino, if not sooner then later. So the only possibility for a rich person in a casino is to make themselves less rich or not rich. I don't get it. I probably never will. For the rest of us, the allure of gambling is the possibility, however remote, that we can "strike it rich" with a jackpot or a run of good luck. That is the bait that keeps us coming back and losing our money over and over. The shot that, one day, we might win enough money to change and better our lives and circumstances. It almost certainly won't happen, but at least it sort of makes sense. But again, what the fuck is a rich person doing there? The only things that ever made the slightest sense were either regular old compulsive behavior or some type of competitive spirit. Particularly when it comes to poker. But still, if you can only make your life worse, why do it at all?

While we're on the subject of casinos, let's go somewhere else that doesn't belong here. Casinos have changed a lot over the decades, and slot machines have become a bigger and bigger part of casinos both in number and from a revenue standpoint. One of the interesting things along the way was the "branding" of a lot of slot machines. That meant a lot of different things. From *I Love Lucy*-themed slots to *Jaws* to *Star Trek* and almost anything else you can think of in pop culture. But the other day I saw one that caught my eye and I'm not even sure why. It was a Genghis Khan slot machine.

In his day, Khan was a pretty busy guy. According to our friends at Google, he was *invariably associated with terrible tales of conquest, destruction, and bloodshed.* But it worked out for him because, at one time, he created and controlled *the largest empire ever to exist.* Because I have a little too much free time, I can't help but imagine Khan brought back from the dead and shown the slot machine created in his honor. Yes, it would take quite a while to bring him up to date on the three trillion things that have changed since the twelfth century, and I just discovered that, yes, there are still people who are fluent in the Old or Classical Mongolian language that our buddy spoke, so we could find someone to translate. I wonder if he would consider it to be an honor to have a slot machine in tribute to him eight hundred years later. These types of thought are one of the better reasons that I am rarely invited to parties.

Anyway, the person who "showed me the ropes" of the casino biz was a good guy with a lifetime of old-school experience. In this case, old school goes back to the days when only Nevada allowed gambling into the years when it was still just Nevada and Atlantic City, New Jersey.

He taught me a bunch of things that still serve me today. "This is a business for intelligent underachievers," he said at a time that it was true. As the industry spread across the country, it became less true. "Dealing in a casino is the equivalent of clean factory work." The truth of that statement has stuck with me over the decades. It is true, but in some ways it's even worse. I would amend it to say, "Dealing in a casino is like clean factory work but with a hostile and angry audience two feet away." You're performing a physically and emotionally taxing, endlessly repetitious ritual for a group of people, almost all of whom are losing their money. Losing money has a tendency to make people just a little . . . well, let's just say assholes. Your day or night is an endless parade of angry assholes. That is the glamorous life of a casino dealer. It is relentless, repetitious, physical, exhausting hard work. That is the truth. And in management of this business, I try very hard to always remember exactly how hard the people under me work. The good ones make it look easy. People who are good at anything make it look easy. But trust me when I tell you that casino life is very, very hard. Burnout is routine.

Do you have any idea how **hard** it is to deal Blackjack? Do you know how **hard** it is just to be a waitress? I don't. I carried some heavy trays of food around almost half a century ago, but I don't know shit. But I know what I see and hear. I see the stains on their uniforms. I see them handling very heavy trays. I see the sweat on their brows. I hear their managers admonish them loud enough for me to hear. I hear older men saying demeaning, sexual things to them. I see them occasionally drop something and then I hear roars of laughter or just screams from customers. I hear customers yell at them because the food took too long or the coffee was cold. I know that it's loud, sweaty, heavy, and often demeaning work that way too often pays way too little. And yet I know that this is nowhere near the bottom rung.

That man pushing the broom. Those women picking fruit. That woman scrubbing the toilet. That man mowing the grass. That factory farm worker waist deep in filth. That factory worker making the same exact repetitive motion minute after minute, hour after hour, day after day, and year after year without end.

For their efforts they receive no respect. The pay they receive is rarely enough for one person to live on, let alone support a partner or a family. **For them I reserve more admiration than I do for the men or women who run Exxon, Apple, or especially Tesla.** These are people whose lives I could never live. I could never survive. I lack the strength and resolve to walk a mile in their shoes. And I know it. Do you?

Once again, I must ask you to pull out that flashlight and shine it on your soul. Do you see these people? Do you *want* to see them? Can you possibly understand how **HARD** life is for them? Do you want to? I don't. I feel much more comfortable when I pretend that they don't exist. Because when I see their lives, it makes me feel like shit to complain about my own. My life is one of ease and wonder compared to any of these people. And yet I am no less a slave to my own need than they are to theirs. My life and work is more comfortable. My job earns more money and a great deal more respect. Yet my life is only slightly more secure than theirs.

In a **Big 4** world, the people who clean our toilets would be revered and ridiculously overpaid. Why? Almost the same reason we now piss on them and pay them nothing. Think about it. Anyone still doing shitty, dirty jobs in a **Big 4** world would be performing an incredible public service. We would respect them in the way we now revere people who serve in the military. Yes, even in a **Big 4** world someone would still have to stand waist deep in chicken guts. But we'd be able to give these amazing people the pay and respect of an NFL quarterback. Exactly as they have **ALWAYS DESERVED**. They might not choose to do this for twenty-five or thirty years like they do now because now they have no other choice but to starve. Maybe they would do it for five years. That's plenty. Stop before it destroys their backs, their lungs, and their souls. Just like a quarterback, you can't and shouldn't do it forever. And they would still suffer. Just like we all do. But it would have a purpose for both them and for society.

Every philosopher will tell you that everyone suffers.

Suffering is central to the human condition. Avoiding suffering is often our most important mission, yet everyone suffers. The factory worker, the waitress, the janitor, the shoeless immigrant. Me, You, Rupert Murdoch (notice that for this part I spelled the fat fuck's name right. Hopefully by the time this book is published he'll be the late Rupret Murdoch). The Kennedy's suffer. The Bushes suffer when Saudi Arabians tell them to and some other times as well. The Nazi Kochs suffer, though not nearly enough. There is a theme here. Can you tell what it is?

That was a rhetorical question. Of course you know. We all suffer. Some of us more, some of us less. Some of us suffer in shit holes while some of us suffer with great food and crown moldings. Some try to suppress their suffering while others choose to wallow in it. Some even set out to inflict suffering on themselves or others. Among those people, some seek some reason they consider valid to inflict suffering. Others are like Rupret and just want to see the world burn and everyone suffer.

The base mindset of almost all of humanity is anxiety and suffering. I can't help but laugh when I read articles that tell us that chronic anxiety is a symptom of modern man or a sick society or culture. Bullshit! Anxiety is bult into us at the molecular level. Our ancient ancestors, the very people whose blood courses through our veins, lived in a constant state of fear and anxiety. That is a large part of why they survived long enough to pass those genes on to us. I assure you that all of their relaxed neighbors became the breakfast of some passing predator. Relaxation and calm were a luxury they couldn't afford. We are born to be nervous, anxious, and to a great extent greedy and unhappy. We are biologically programmed to always want more, to never be satisfied with what we have. We are machines programmed to eat, fuck, and gather as many things as possible to make sure we can continue to eat and fuck. Happiness and satisfaction are most definitely and completely abnormal. We are biologically programmed to run around the planet with the only goal being to survive to continue running around the planet. And to pass these genes on to others so that they can run around the planet for a while.

But just like every other instinct, we can learn to rise above it. Humans certainly haven't stopped evolving. And the **Big 4** is what will give us that chance to rise above what we are and be what we can be.

For argument's sake, let's say that the vast majority of people would like to reduce suffering. Not just their own, but everybody's. I am among those people in both ways. I would like to suffer less AND I would like to see everybody else suffer less. If you have somehow muddled this far into this book, then I would be willing to bet that you agree with me.

I believe that universal **Big 4**, or **4 For All**, would be the best way to improve the human experience to the point where we would have the chance to endure the least possible amount of suffering.

There may be some validity to some thoughts that you may have just had somewhere along the way in reading the last couple of pages, just like I did as I wrote them. Is not some suffering necessary? Are not some types of suffering good in some way? Is it possible that suffering may motivate us to do things that improve our lives or the lives of others? Is suffering useful in some spiritual way to fully realize ourselves? Honestly, I don't know. But I know of one form of almost completely worthless suffering that would be greatly reduced in a universal **Big 4** world.

12

———

FEAR

Do you live every moment with fear that if things go wrong, you and your family will be homeless and hungry? I do. It's not on my mind constantly, but it's almost impossible to grasp how much of my behavior is influenced by that thought. It has influenced almost every decision I have made in my life. It has influenced almost every decision you have made, every decision our parents made for us, and every decision we make for our children. It's almost impossible to measure how different life would be without that fear. We are all born hitting the ground running and always just for the basic right to exist. To assure the **Big 4**. It might be easier to figure out what human behavior is NOT based on the **Big 4**.

There is one thing I am sure about. It's massive. It would involve every one of those social sciences listed above. There are times I think that grasping the concept is harder than actually achieving the goal. I know that's not true. But I also know that grasping the concept is a crucial step in the right direction. Arguably the first step. So let's start with a not-so-short list of questions to get us all started, myself included:

- How much of our time and attention is devoted to our need to provide the **Big 4**?
- What would we teach our children in school if the **Big 4** were not the primary goal?
- What would we teach each other?
- What would we do with our time if we did not need to spend that time in pursuit of the **Big 4**?
- Would we become lazy and uninspired if our basic needs were guaranteed?
- Would we lack curiosity, creativity, and any entrepreneurial desires?
- This is a big one. How do we earn self-respect and a sense of worth in a world that does not directly require our services? We will have the time and opportunity to acquire new skills, new hobbies. Perhaps that will restore a sense of self-worth.
- Would there ever be another war?
- Where would YOU be? At work? Would you be married? If you are married now, do you think you would have been married at all in a **Big 4** world? If yes, do you think you would be with the same person that you're married to now? Do you have kids? Would you have had more or fewer kids in a **Big 4** world? If you don't have kids, might you have had them in a **Big 4** world?
- What about gratitude? Forgive me. I'm just sticking this in here because I don't know what else to do with it. I am aware that most of this book so far has been a complaint in one form or another. But I am grateful for some things. There was a man I used to work with that I didn't like. Not that he was a terrible person, but he was kind of a schemy, sleazy, and selfish sort of dirt ball. Try to imagine Uncle Fester from *The Addams Family* but not funny. This guy is

every bit as bald but fatter and younger. These days I
bump into him every once in a while. It's not
horrible. He hasn't yet tried to stab me. He's not
openly hostile. He's just an annoying douche. Every
time I see him, I am grateful—grateful for the times
that I DON'T see him. I am very appreciative and
grateful for his absence.

While we are talking fear, there is something I've been
thinking about for a while now. We all know that the rich are
getting much richer and the poor are getting much poorer. We
also know that every day more and more Americans are slip-
ping off the middle-class life raft into the freezing water of
poverty. The takeaway from this is that every day there are
fewer and fewer people with any money to spend, let alone any
so-called disposable income.

So stay with me a second because we are going to take that
truth in another direction entirely. Most of the things that
entertain us are free or almost free. TV, sports on TV, social
media like YouTube and TikTok, games on your phone, and a
bunch of other things I'm not thinking of at the moment. Have
you ever asked yourself why these things are free? Well, even if
you didn't ask, the answer is **eyeballs**.

Eyeballs pay for our entertainment. The more eyeballs
something gets, the more money it makes. From your favorite
TV shows to social media "influencers." The revenue made is in
direct proportion to how many people use those eyeballs to
watch. Why? Because once they have your attention, they can
try to sell you things. Commercials on TV, ads on your favorite
games, or that sales pitch you have to sit through before you
can click "skip ad" and get to the video you want to watch.

But here's what worries me. All of it is predicated on the
idea that your attention, your **eyeballs**, are worth something.
What will happen when the day comes that so many of us are

so poor that our eyeballs are worthless to the advertisers. It may be a while yet, but I assure you that day will come. We are well on the way. And then all hell is going to break loose. Because there will be no incentive for anyone to give you anything for your attention. You want to watch the Super Bowl? Fuck you! Pay for it. You want to play a game on your phone? Fuck you! Pay for it. Yes, I know that some things are already a pay/ad hybrid. But in the world that is coming, almost all media, all broadcasting, and all the sports and games will have to be paid for. Because most of our eyeballs will be worthless. Because we don't have the money to buy the toe fungus remedy they're peddling on Fox News in between the lies about the election they were proven to have knowingly told.

This may not sound like a big deal, but I assure you it is. But maybe I'm wrong. After all, even poor people got talked into paying for and schlepping the water that otherwise comes out of their faucets. So maybe there won't be a revolt when the poor have to pay to watch the Super Bowl or The Real Housewives of Shitsville. Or maybe they will. One thing is for sure: As the rest of the middle class evaporates into poverty, weirdness won't be far behind.

Everything above is just the tippiest tip of the iceberg. I'm going to try a scattershot approach to trying to cross the moat of my own brain and some of you people.

Here's a big one: healthcare.

13

HEALTHCARE?

What's with the question mark? Why healthcare with a question mark? There is a good answer, but I promise you you're not going to like it. Not unless you happen to be an HMO executive or a mental patient. The reason for the question mark is simple. There is no **healthcare** in the United States. There is only a **healthcare business**.

You will hear people say that healthcare in the United States is "broken." There are only two kinds of people that would say that they are satisfied with the healthcare system.

1. People who have never been sick and have never met anyone who was, and
2. People who profit from the system as it is. There is almost no one in the first group.

People who say the healthcare system is broken are wrong and completely missing the point. It's not "broken." It perfectly performs the function it was specifically created to do: **ENHANCE SHAREHOLDER VALUE.** Any actual healthcare that is performed is incidental, performative, and counterproductive to the purposes of the **healthcare business.**

The reason for this is yet another dry but very important economic term: perverse incentives.

This means that almost every incentive to the healthcare business is at odds with actual healthcare and patients. We will start with the biggest and most glaring problem. If you are an HMO, how do you make money? How do you enhance shareholder value? If you are the CEO of an HMO, let's call it KleptoCare. The way you make money is by charging as much as you possibly can and then delivering as little healthcare as you possibly can.

Think about it. Anytime a customer receives any care, they are costing your shareholders money. It is your job, your fiduciary duty, your sworn responsibility to maximize your revenue and minimize your expenses. Anyone receiving any healthcare of any kind is an expense. It is your job to prevent expenses in any and every legal way. And since healthcare lobbyists own and control the government (see our old economic friend regulatory capture) you have many legal tools at your disposal to prevent healthcare from taking place and keeping expenses low for KleptoCare.

TIMEOUT: We need to take a break for a moment. As I am researching and writing this, I began to have a sinking feeling and the first stirrings of nausea. As I write this, I am a relatively healthy sixty-year-old with a thoroughly torn meniscus and a host of other problems induced by a lifetime of alleged athletic pursuits. Also, due to a faulty seatbelt, I took an unscheduled trip where my head slammed into the ceiling of a seaplane. Somehow I failed to die doing this, though for a while there I wish I had. Nevertheless, I remain alive, with hips, back, shoulder, elbow, and knees in various stages of decay. All cause some pain. But nothing I can't handle for now. And here's where the nausea starts. I know that if I am lucky enough to continue to live, sooner or later I'm going to need a lot more healthcare than I need now. And I know that these motherfuckers are going to try and kill me—and you—because it is their job.

OK, so at this point you may be saying to yourself, "Hey, fuck it. Why don't I just quit my job as CEO at KleptoCare? You could, but it wouldn't matter. The new CEO would face the same set of perverse incentives. Or worse, he might actually enjoy the work. Not unlike the Catholic Church, jobs like that attract the deeply sick. They attract sociopaths like moths to a flame. He may love the power of life and death. He may actually enjoy the torture they put their customers through.

So as I said. You, as CEO of KleptoCare have any number of ways to slow down or completely stop the healthcare process. All the while your sick victim grows ever sicker and less able to jump through the hoops that you hold above their heads. Just a little too high for them to jump through.

You, as CEO, have a wide range of tools with which to perform your fuckery on sick, confused practically defenseless victims. But most of them fall under two main categories. For public view they sound almost harmless and positive. Um . . . no. Before I begin here, you should know that these horrible things you are about to see have ALL been verified and proven through the court records of any number of cases. The point is that it's true. Ugly, but true. Steel your resolve and read on.

- **Gatekeeping:** Sounds benign-ish, but no. It's exactly as it sounds. Someone at the gate to make sure a sick person doesn't accidentally sneak past the gate and get some actual care. One of the big parts of gatekeeping is *referrals*. Let's say the victim needs to see a specialist. For argument's sake, let's say an oncologist because they think this loser just might have some form of cancer. Now anyone with at least one non-malignant brain cell knows they need to see an oncologist. But not you, CEO of KleptoCare. You are going to require the patient to see his primary care physician (PCP) in order to request a referral before even thinking of seeing an oncologist. Now hold on a second. Isn't this contrary to my whole big speech "every visit costs the shareholders . . . blah, blah, blah"? It's true, but for your company it's worth it for a bunch of reasons. First of all, who knows how long it might take our victim to even get the appointment. Then once they do, the office will make them wait a couple more hours. Then, they screw up the actual referral a whole bunch of times to slow the victim down again. Plus, the PCP is completely in your (CEO) pocket. You are probably getting this guy to see the victim just for the cost of the co-pay you force on your victims. So it's probably not costing your company anything to plop the victim into his office. And as a group, you virtually own them—the PCPs I mean. You make them take on hundreds of patients to scratch out a living. You weigh them down with paperwork just like you do your retail victims. You keep those fucken doctors on a short leash and wearing roller skates, dashing from one victim to the next in packed, chaotic settings to keep the whole process barely moving at a snail's pace, generating mountains of paperwork and red tape at every stop. All to keep expenses low. Now remember, you're dealing with a sick and probably terrified victim. They might not even get past even those first obstacles. They might give up. They might die. Both of which help you (the CEO) to keep costs down. Oh, by the way, your little pet doctor might not even give the victim the referral they need. Because you (the CEO) have given the doctors very limited quotas of how many referrals they can hand out and how many procedures they can approve. The victim can of course appeal the decision, but they may spend hours more on the phone trying to get the right person, and even then, they might be denied. If they're lucky, they'll win the right to wait to see another doctor who may or may not approve their referral once they repeat the process. Or not. Or maybe, hopefully for you, the CEO, they just die or give up. These fucken sick people. Don't they understand how much money they might cost your shareholders if they hang in there and fight hard enough to eventually get some healthcare? Disgusting! Sick people are so . . . well . . . sick.

- **Utilization Management:** Again, sounds pretty benign, right? Unlike the victim's tumor. But it's really your best tool for slowing down, stopping, or killing those annoying patients that keep trying to cost KleptoCare money. Some of these victims are pretty effective and motivated by that whole "dying" thing. You, as CEO, can't understand why they are so difficult about things. After all, it's not a REAL problem. It's not as if you (the CEO) have cancer or anything like that. You feel just fine. You might even take the yacht out this weekend. So you have three great friends in this "utilization management" thing. First you have co-pays. With help from your "employees" in government, you have made the victims' copays rise to the point that they pay for a huge percentage of what used to be KleptoCare's liabilities. Even for some surgeries you have used copays, deductibles, and negotiations with providers to make it so that none of KleptoCare's money is spent. The actual procedure is performed for the amount of the patient's copay. Next you have "prior authorization." This is the fun one because you and KleptoCare get to play doctor. See, the doctor says this stupid patient "needs" something expensive— let's say a CAT scan. Just because he has MD after his name doesn't mean he gets to decide. You (CEO of KleptoCare) decide that that expensive test is not allowed. And by the way, you are probably going to go after that stupid spendthrift doctor who is probably over his quota and needs to be put in his place. I know somebody out there might be saying, "Now hold on just one cotton-pickin' minute! You can't overrule the doctor. That would be practicing medicine without a god damn License!" Oh, you silly rube. Let me kindly explain. **WE OWN THE GOVERNMENT! WE WILL PRACTICE MEDICINE WITHOUT A LICENSE WHENEVER WE GOD DAMN PLEASE. IN EVERY STATE. AND THERE IS NOT A THING YOU CAN DO ABOUT IT. NOW GET BACK TO WORK BEFORE I CALL YOUR BOSS AND TELL HIM YOU'VE BEEN HARASSING US ON THEIR COMPANY TIME!** So now for the victim, the whole merry-go-round starts up again. They can get back on the phone for a few hours to reach someone and beg you (remember, you are still CEO of KleptoCare) to allow their potentially lifesaving procedure, once again giving the victim the option of just giving up or hopefully dying. Here's the last one—deductibles. So those are really fun and useful. You now structure most of your plans to include deductibles. What it actually means is that KleptoCare doesn't even begin to pay a dime until the victims have already spent thousands out of their own pockets in any given timeframe. As CEO, you can't help but have a little giggle. Because you know that at the end of the day you've got it worked out that even if those stupid victims actually somehow manage to wrangle a bit of healthcare, KleptoCare probably still didn't have to spend a dime. You have performed your job admirably. Because when it comes right down to it, your victims aren't even paying for "insurance." In reality, they are quite comically paying for a little plastic card and the right to **say that they have health insurance.** Because you, you little genius, worked it out so that KleptoCare almost never actually pays for anything. You just sit by and watch the victims' premiums roll in and your stock options add up.

I apologize a little bit for casting you in the role of the villain. But it was for a good reason. You are probably a nice person. You would never do all those things that have to be done as the CEO of KleptoCare. But if you didn't, you would be immediately fired and replaced with someone who would. And the board would have to fire you. It's their job. It's more than their job, it's their sworn fiduciary duty. Even they are in a no-win situation. If they keep you, they have violated their share-holders' trust. It would actually be morally wrong for them not to fire you. All choices lead to evil. That is why:

For-profit healthcare is an abomination, and will always lead to death, poverty, and humiliation.

But yes, it is broken. And we are going to try to fix it later on. See you then.

14

DRUGS

This one is as big as it is multifaceted. Let's talk drugs and alcohol. This particular subject touches on so many other issues that it's worth starting with this and working through it.

With the exception of the brief prohibition period, alcohol has been legal in the United States and more or less legal in the rest of the non-Muslim world. Tobacco and caffeine use has always been legal in the U.S. and probably the rest of the world. I'm not going to bother looking it up because really, who gives a shit? All three are mood-altering drugs. There's another long list of mood-altering drugs that are legal but require a prescription. We're talking opioids, benzos, amphetamines, barbiturates, the ones for when your toes are a bit yellow, and a whole bunch more.

Then there is a long list of illegal drugs. And let's not forget weed, which has become mostly legal and, when not explicitly legal, is mostly ignored by the law (unless you are black, of course).

OK. Before we get into it, I want to mention a lesson taught to me by one of the most intuitive people I have ever known personally. This being true reinforces the notion that everyone can contribute something worth knowing. Her thought was this: She was working in a convenience store and, one day, she came home and told me something I had never thought of before but is actually quite obvious once you think about it. Ninety-nine percent of her store's sales were of addictive and/or mood-altering products. That ninety-nine percent included cigarettes and other nicotine products, coffee, energy drinks (addictive caffeine delivery vehicles), beer and other alcohol products, gambling in the form of lottery tickets (not a substance but a dopamine-producing "vice"), foods high in fat, sugar, and salt (other than sugar, these can't be classified as "drugs," but they are clearly addictive), and gasoline (addictive in a larger social sense).

OK, how do we tie up all the tendrils of this issue, and how does it relate to the overall issue of the **Big 4**. Where to start? First of all, how does society choose which category a particular substance belongs in? Remember, we have three to choose from: legal, illegal, or prescription. Let's try to start figuring this out. Why was weed illegal for over a century but only now beginning to be legal and openly accepted? The product itself has not changed. Well, actually it has changed a lot, but not in a way that should have made it more likely to be legal. Marijuana in its various forms is exponentially more potent than it has ever been. I still don't believe that it is particularly dangerous, but it is way more powerful and addictive than ever (but still not particularly physically addictive).

When Colorado legalized weed a few years ago, emergency room visits went through the roof. The reason, it turns out, was edibles. Unlike smoking a joint or a bong, edibles take at least thirty minutes to kick in. So you got this guy who smokes weed regularly and has built up a pretty good tolerance to its effects. One day he decides to get some gummies. He eats one and doesn't feel a thing, as opposed to when he smokes, he starts to feel high as soon as he gets done coughing. But with the gummies, nothing. So he eats another one. Still nothing. "What the fuck?!" he thinks and eats one more thinking that this whole thing is bullshit and the god damn things don't work. He got ripped off. An hour later, he is sitting in the emergency room sweating his tits off with his blood pressure through the roof. He is also thinking how nice it would be to have a glass of chocolate milk and some Cheetos. He is high as fuck.

The point is that weed, while still relatively harmless and most definitely less harmful than alcohol, has become worse for people, even as it gained legal and social acceptance. So obviously there is more going on here than just harm mitigation.

Weed was illegal for a century because it had two very powerful enemies: the surprisingly potent alcohol sellers lobby and the ever-present gargantuan influence of the Big Pharmaceutical companies. Weed has the unfortunate tendency to help treat things that Big Pharma makes a boatload of money slinging. Let's just pick one class of drugs, benzos. The drugs we all know as Xanax, Valium, Ativan, and Librium, just to name a few. Some conservative estimates are that Big Pharma has made more than $100 billion just by selling benzos. That's enough to make Hector Salamanca and Pablo Escobar blush. Remember that's just one class of drugs. One hundred billion is enough to buy and sell every judge, every member of Congress, and every Prius-driving employee of the FDA since the 1850s, with more than enough left over to buy me, you, your more attractive younger sister, and three popes, just for starters. And that's just one fucken class of drugs. Legal weed disrupts a shitload of other pain killers, blood pressure pills, anxiety drugs, and god knows what else. Legal weed is so disruptive to Big Pharma profits that it is a minor miracle that it ever became legal. The success of legalized marijuana, despite the massive forces arrayed against it, brings me feelings of hope that if enough people are motivated, we can overcome. Reference and salute to Dr. King fully intended.

So the pharmaceutical industry had a huge, vested interest in keeping weed illegal. And they did for over a century. Am I the only one who has noticed that it has been a long time since modern medicine has "cured" anything? They have done a wonderful job of "treating" things. But actual cures just don't seem to be on the menu. Treating things, as it so happens, is wonderfully profitable for Big Pharma. Curing, not so much. Polio killed and crippled millions. We cured it. Smallpox killed millions. We cured it. AIDS killed millions. We "treat" it. With ridiculously expensive and profitable pills that have to be taken every day. I am not outright saying that the industry has abandoned one-shot, reasonably profitable "cures" in favor of wildly profitable ongoing "treatments," but it sure as fuck looks like it. There are a handful of ailments that cause misery and/or death in a massive portion of our population. But we don't cure high blood pressure, diabetes, arthritis, asthma, or cancer. Just for a minute, consider how much human suffering would evaporate if we "cured" cancer. Now consider how much "profit" would be lost by Big Pharma. We're talking NASA numbers here. But for now, we "treat" cancer and other life-threatening ailments in incredibly expensive and extremely profitable ways. Now I'm not pointing my finger and saying there is some conspiracy holding the industry back for the purpose of making obscene profit by selling their victims daily treatments. But let's be honest, it sure as shit looks that way. Both polio and smallpox were completely dispatched before the first cell phone. Technology sure does seem to have stalled when it comes to finding "cures" for the most common and deadly things that ail us . . . hmm.

Before I get away from our lovely, moral, caring and empathy-filled friends over at the pharmaceutical industry, let's talk about their almost always humorous television commercials.

Through the brave, selfless, and caring lobbying by the industry, it became legal for them to advertise drugs on television.

In 1997, the drug makers paid off the FDA to allow them to air commercials on television. To this day, the only other countries that allow that are Brazil and New Zealand. Unlike the U.S., they have very strict guidelines as to what they can advertise and how they can do it. Here there are virtually no rules. They are free to advertise any old shit to any old moron.

Let's take a step back for a moment. Why would they even want to? Presumably, if one of those human creatures had a medical problem, they would go to one of those doctor people. And presumably the doctor person would treat them and give them a prescription for medication to solve the problem if they needed it. So why would there be any reason for a drug company to want to reach and manipulate potential patients directly? On the surface, it makes no sense. Unless, of course, you are trying to sell them things they didn't know they need or SELL THEM THINGS THEY DON'T REALLY NEED.

Let's consider the first point first. It's slightly (but only slightly) less evil. The potential patient doesn't know they need the drug, or perhaps it's an all-new drug that cures, or way more likely "treats," an existing problem. This still makes zero sense. If a patient has a problem, surely any competent doctor would know of the new treatment and prescribe it. Also, any competent and trustworthy doctor would not prescribe a medication if it doesn't work or if the patient doesn't need it. So let's look at the next point: They are trying to sell patients something they don't need. Well bless their little corporate lowlife hearts. Why would they try to sell something to someone they don't need? And what's more, why would any doctor follow through and prescribe a drug to a patient that they don't need?

We have arrived at Scumbag Central. Not only do the drug companies run commercials to sell the patients on dubious, unnecessary, and sometimes dangerous drugs they don't need, but the last part of the puzzle is that they grease up the doctors with things such as (it is important for you to know at this point that this is all completely true and documented, although I wish it weren't) fully paid vacations, golf outings, straight up cash payments, and—last but not least . . . drum roll, please—hand jobs, blow jobs, and full-on sexual favors for the doctor from the pharmaceutical sales reps. These things are true and well documented, although there are some odd white, crusty stains on some of the documents.

If you visit a doctor with any frequency, I am sure you have seen them. Attractive young women (and sometimes men), usually pulling a small rolling briefcase, going in and out of doctors' offices all across our great nation. Each pharmaceutical company employs armies of sales reps, many of whom are simply prostitutes in pantsuits. Why would you need to "market" pharmaceuticals at all? Wouldn't you think that it is as simple as a doctor examining a patient and determining what drugs, if any, are necessary? And to be honest, a little marketing makes sense. Different companies make similar items with similar efficacies, so why not try to give your brand a bit of a competitive edge? I get that.

But that's not what they do, and that's not what actually happens in the real world. You see, the goal of all pharmaceutical companies is exactly the same as that of every other corporation. Let's not forget our old friend **ENHANCE SHAREHOLDER VALUE.** That means they can't, don't, and won't ever give a flying fuck about the doctor, patient, or anybody else. The only goal is to sell, sell, sell. You will see exactly that in a ton of documentary films, many of which are about our very special and dear friends over at Purdue Pharmaceuticals. Owned and operated by the also very well-documented Sackler family.

They are by no means the only culprits. But this one family

basically created the opioid epidemic by getting the FDA to label their brand of opioids, Oxycontin, as non-addictive. In a way it's funny. It would be funnier had it not caused millions of people to die and millions of others to go broke or be imprisoned. But the reason I think it's funny is because the world has known that opium in any form is ridiculously and heartbreakingly addictive since at least the twelfth century. Yup, even Genghis Khan knew opium is addictive. I'm imaging a headline: "Opium is addictive, who knew?" What a fucken joke. What a cruel, murderous, heartless devastating joke.

Yet Purdue managed to get the FDA to label Oxycontin as non-addictive. I am quite sure they achieved this objective with a straight face and a firm handshake. With this green light, doctors began doling out opioids to virtually anyone who walked by like they were M&M's. Personally, I have a really shitty knee that appears god awful in an MRI. I am not joking when I say that multiple doctors practically begged me to take Oxycontin. And I did. I consider myself extremely fortunate that the second time I took one, I projectile vomited. Every ensuing attempt to take it also ended with more projectile vomiting. There is not a single shred of doubt in my mind that if I could have kept it down, I would have become addicted. Just like dozens of people I know. Or knew, actually, because some are dead from overdoses, and those that aren't are addicted.

I'm looking at the last couple of paragraphs I have just written and wish to all that is holy that I was making this shit up. It can't be real. Unfortunately for you, me, and millions of others, its real. The one and only mandate at Purdue was to sell, sell, sell Oxycontin. There are videos in court records proving exactly that. And they did sell, sell, sell. Creating untold millions of addicts, inmates, debtors, and corpses. I don't believe there is a single American alive today that hasn't felt the consequences of this unholy crime. Yet not a single person at Purdue or any of the other Big Pharmaceuticals that rode the wave has served even a single moment in jail. The same cannot be said of many of the newly created addicts. They went to prison for a variety of different crimes connected to their addiction. In fact, there was a giant wave of drug-related crime that swept over America in Purdue's wake that still has not yet abated. Many of the addicted had no choice but to turn to illegal alternatives such as heroin and fentanyl.

Because now the legal pendulum has swung so far back the other way that actual pain patients, who can't function without their legitimately needed medication, can no longer get it. And if they do somehow legally beg and plead for it from understandably legally gun-shy doctors, they are treated as addicts and criminals. In other words, we have now made it so that the only people who can't get it are the poor bastards that actually legitimately need it and had used it correctly and legally. Because opium-derived products do really have a legitimate and proper use for the seriously wounded or dying. For many people it is the pain medication of last resort. And all we've done is make life immeasurably worse for the people who truly need it. Well done, America. Well done, Purdue. Well done, indeed.

All of these new opium addicts led some crafty folk to come up with the synthetic version of opium: fentanyl. It is hundreds of times more powerful than any naturally derived opioid. It's also cheap to produce and small and easy to transport and conceal. And best of all, it is easily added to gin up the potency of any number of other substances. There's just one teensy-weensy problem. Those pesky and annoying dead people. Millions of them dead worldwide from fentanyl. This stuff is so absurdly powerful that cops have died just from handling it with bare hands. Most of the people dying from it didn't even know they were buying it. A lot of them thought they were buying weed, benzos, or coke. Relatively benign substances.

Sadly, not knowing what they were buying doesn't make them any less dead.

I thought twice about including statins in this section. I actually thought about it three times or more. And as depressing as it is, I decided to include it. The reason being that I spent a ridiculous amount of time researching and it just seemed a waste. Depression-era thinking is still part of me and "waste not, want not" still courses through my veins. And even that is part of the story because it's almost impossible to do real research when it comes to the pharmaceutical industry. Almost everywhere you look for facts, you will find the fingerprints of the industry. Finding independent studies, results, and meaningful numbers was like trying to find a doctor that *wasn't* trying to give you oxycontin in 2012. That was the year that 255 million oxycontin prescriptions were written. That's 81.3 per 100 persons. It is literally incomprehensible.

But because I went through so much trouble, let's talk statins, an alleged anti-cholesterol drug. It is prescribed to reduce levels of "bad" LDL cholesterol that is linked to increased risk of heart attack and stroke. The first of them was Pfizer's Lipitor. Pfizer had patent protection on Lipitor for fifteen years. During those years, it generated $131 billion in sales. Yes, billion. Keep in mind, that is one drug from one manufacturer. There are various statins made by many companies, and now a whole bunch of generic versions are available. It's not at all hyperbolic to say that it is likely that more than $1 trillion have been made selling statins. Here's the thing, I'm not sure they work. You can find hundreds of studies funded by drug companies that say they work. You could also get Hitler to read the four questions at your Passover celebration. Both are equally valid. I couldn't find any independent study to support the efficacy of statins and, please believe me, I tried. Do they work? I'm still not sure. But there is very good, very real reason to doubt it.

As awful as it is, the thought that they don't work doesn't imply any conspiracy. The people who make and sell them may very well believe that they work. Confirmation bias is as real for them as it is for you and me. As George said to Jerry on *Seinfeld*, "Remember, Jerry, it's not a lie if you believe it yourself." So you don't have to imagine mustache-twirling, villainous drug makers defrauding the forty percent of the country that takes some form of statin. But does it really matter? If they don't work, they totally fucked a whole lot of people. From the National Library of Medicine, part of the U.S. government's National Institutes of Health:

> A double-blind placebo-controlled trial of lovastatin's effect on cognitive functioning and mood showed detrimental effects on cognitive performance on four neuropsychological tests assessing attention, working memory, and overall mental efficiency. A follow up double blind, randomized trial found a significantly worsened learning effect in participants taking statins compared to placebo. The participants on statins were not able to learn from prior experiences as well as those on placebo. The strength of evidence is heightened by the randomization and controlled structure in these studies . . .

Just in case you fell asleep halfway through that quote, basically the drug makes you stupid. And that was my own exact experience with a statin some twenty years ago. I took it for about three months. I felt stupid. Or more stupid, if you prefer. The truth is that it definitely affected my cognitive abilities so much that it was noticeable to myself and others. I got off the drug and, within two weeks, I began to feel normal again. Well, normal for me anyway. I got my cholesterol and weight down through a combination of eating slightly less shittily, walking a fair bit, and basically getting older and having less of an appetite. I also heard and took the only piece of diet advice most of us will ever need: **Don't eat if you aren't hungry.**

I know, it sounds ridiculous, but if you really stop to think about it, how often do you eat when you aren't hungry? We as a species eat for any number of reasons, but a lot of it is socialized. Cake at the office, inhaling a quart of ice cream because some asshole wrote a book saying that HMOs are trying to kill you and it upset you. Maybe it's just **time** to eat. Whatever. Just try to eat only when you are hungry, and you will probably be OK. You're welcome.

ALERT! TWO COMPLETELY SPECULATIVE MUSINGS FORTHCOMING:

It occurs to me that statins are a big part of the reason that it seems people in general are getting dumber. It also occurs to me that there is a giant overlap in demographics among Trump voters and statin users. Stranger things have most certainly happened and might even be happening right now, as you read about . . .

Chiropractors. An industry that exists solely by virtue of cognitive dissonance and confirmation bias. It is nonsense. And occasionally very dangerous nonsense. But if you subject a million chiropractors to a lie detector test and ask them if their "adjustments" help, I bet almost all of them would pass. It's not a lie, Jerry, because they believe it. And it probably does work a little bit, once in a while. But it's simply because someone is caring for and about the patient. Just the thought of that alone has been proven to help some of us fragile and vulnerable humans.

15

DRUGS AND RACE

If you were foolish enough to allow yourself to have been born black, there are an enormous set of consequences, not the least of which is this: In the 1970s, Richard Nixon declared war on drugs. It is extremely well documented that his publicly announced "War on Drugs" was a privately voiced war on, as he put it, "niggers and hippies." Turns out that, for Nixon, a war on drugs was a pretty convenient way to lock up and disenfranchise people you don't like and certainly don't want anywhere near a voting booth.

What Nixon started, our boy Reagan ran with. Again, this is well documented and completely true. Reagan had Nancy out there running the wildly successful (please note sarcasm) "Just Say No" anti-drug campaign. At the same time, he cut a deal with Nicaraguan "Contras" who were fighting the damn commies that took over Nicaragua. Reagan financed the *Contras* war by allowing them to freely import crack into the U.S., laser focused on communities of color. At the same time, the war on drugs was cranked up with absurdly harsh penalties for even tiny amounts of crack. It was a perfect plan of killing two birds with one stone. Fight the commies and destroy black communities and lock up the survivors. He actually got three birds with that stone. Let's not forget the money he received from the private prison industry for giving them victims to lock up. It almost makes me wish there was a hell for Reagan and his people to burn in. I'm not going to bore you with too much more of this shit. It's disgusting. Here are just a few numbers to clear things up:

In 1960, 346,000 people were incarcerated in the United States. Sixty-five percent were black.

In 2010, 2,270,142 people were incarcerated in the United States. Black Americans were incarcerated at a rate of 4,347 per 100,000 residents, compared to a rate of 678 per 100,000 for white Americans. Yeah, if someone were in jail in 2010, it's almost seven times as likely that they were black. And let's not forget that, overall, we locked up more than nine times as many people as a half century earlier. Did Americans just become lawless assholes during that half a century? Or was there something else in play?

Just for the sake of comparison. About a quarter of the people locked up in the **whole world** were locked up in the Land of the Free. That's right. The good old U.S. of A. We are four percent of the world population and have twenty-five percent of the world's prisoners. Lol. Land of the Free indeed. Well, it is a profitable business. If the industry plays their cards right and buys the right government folks, maybe we can lock up half our people and get the other half to pay for it. A man can dream. But back to business. Pardon the pun.

It's all a giant Jim Crow-ish clusterfuck.

But what does any of this have to do with the **Big 4**?

Well, I can't prove any of this, but if we were born into a Big 4 world, I would like to think we would be less racist.

I would like to think we would be less likely to use drugs.

I know we would be less likely to imprison people for drug use.

I know that the imperial legal and illegal drug cartels would have less or no power to corrupt.

I know the drug companies would not exist in their current grotesque form.

I know remaining drug companies would have far less perverse incentive to blow doctors and peddle dangerous shit to enhance shareholder value.

I know private prisons would not exist.

I know that without private prisons there would be no incentive to "lock 'em up and throw away the key."

I know that the incentive to do shitty things in general would be dramatically reduced. Anecdotally, of course, but in a **4 For All** world, would anybody really bother to:

- Mug somebody?
- Perform a home-invasion robbery?
- Sell heroin?
- Blow doctors to prescribe their company's drugs?
- Shoot a clerk while robbing a convenience store?
- Fuck people for money or fuck people for money? (Notice how clever it was to describe two very different things with the exact same words.)
- (In case you didn't get the previous very cleverly constructed joke) **Engage in prostitution?** This is a complete and total guess, but I think there would still be a bit of prostitution across the gender spectrum. The reason being that I don't think that all prostitution is completely and strictly monetarily transactional. I think some people just really like to fuck. Some people like the idea that someone is willing to pay them for any range of sexual activities. In other words, it's a power thing that brings sexual satisfaction. In some people, it might rise to the level of addiction or otherwise clinically harmful urges,

but who am I to say what is "harmful" in a sexual context? As long as everyone consents and there are no kids or animals involved, I say go to it. And good luck!

- Tell their boss that their hair isn't really thinning that much when it is actually thinning, and quite badly?
- Study or work at something they hate? (Like law. Ninety percent of the lawyers I know who hate it.)
- Drive aggressively, dangerously, or recklessly to avoid being late for work?

Let's take a break for a bit. Sooner or later, we need to discuss all seven components of the **Big 4**

I've been carrying on for quite a while now about the **Big 4** and **4 For All**. I'm not backing away from any of it, and we are going to get around to changing and fixing the world. But for the moment let's work on a couple of things.

First of all, when I say the four, it conflates the importance of food and clothing next to housing, energy, and education. It's not that all of them aren't important. It's more about the fact that two of them won't be much of a problem to conquer. Food and clothing are absolutely vital. But to provide them universally won't be anywhere near as problematic as the issues of universal housing, education, water, energy, and healthcare.

Food and clothing are relatively cheap in the big picture. Not that it wouldn't be a big deal to feed and clothe everybody. But those two would be a tiny fraction of the mountains we would need to move to assure the remaining necessities for everyone. So let's talk water.

16

———

WATER

We tend to mentally lump food and water together. But in terms of assuring them to everyone, it would be very, very different. Water is a big fucken deal and there a lot of pieces to the puzzle. Water for everyone would be a surprisingly complex issue. And a couple of those issues brings up things that are nearly as repulsive as the whole healthcare, drugs, religion, and guns stuff. As usual, there is a whole lot of corporate fuckery going on. Let's start with that.

BOTTLED WATER AND THE END OF THE WORLD

In 1970, almost no Americans drank bottled water. The number of bottles sold was so close to zero as to effectively **be** zero. In 2020, more than forty billion plastic bottles of bottled water were sold in the U.S.

I think we can all agree that this is a pretty significant difference, zero per year to forty billion per year in half a century is a pretty big difference. Let's try to figure out why and what it means.

You might think that something went drastically wrong

with our municipal water supplies. I actually thought that something went drastically wrong with our municipal water supplies. We would both be wrong. By every standard, municipal water is the best it has ever been by every measure of purity, safety, and taste. Really. It's true. I was so surprised that I checked a bunch of different sources because I thought it had to be a mistake. It's not a mistake. Overall, municipal water supplies are the best they have ever been. Yes, there have been some very well-publicized exceptions. Flint, Michigan immediately springs to mind (pardon the pun). But no, nothing has gone drastically wrong with our municipal water supplies. They probably will soon have problems, as Flint so dramatically demonstrated, as cash-strapped cities, counties, and states are so busy giving tax cuts to billionaires and corporations that they don't have the money to safeguard, upgrade, and modernize our water systems. But for the moment, they are still primarily OK.

In fact, the real problem is that something has gone drastically right. Unfortunately, in this case, it was marketing and advertising. The history of environmental and medical disaster caused by bottled water is really a simultaneous history of marketing.

It started with Perrier in the early 1980s marketing its water as an ultra-premium brand for the affluent. The advertising for Perrier was remarkably, and to me inexplicably, successful. Their success led to imitators like Evian, Fiji, San Pellegrino, and Miller Lite. I'm kidding about Miller Lite because, according to my research, it is beer. But it gives me the chance to insert one of my favorite jokes. Ready? *How is Miller Lite like having sex in a canoe? They are both fucking close to water.* The truth is Miller Lite really isn't bad. I'll even drink one or two now and again with a lime, so please don't sue me. But the thing Perrier and its competitors had in common was that they sold their water as a very special kind from a very special place.

All of it was nonsense. But wildly successful nonsense and it became a kind of virtue and wealth signaling among the prominent.

But the real growth and the real damage began when the big boys jumped in the game in the 1990s. The Coca-Cola Company introduced Dasani and Pepsico blessed the world with Aquafina. As you might expect, it supercharged the industry and sales of water in plastic bottles soared right into our landfills and our bodies. More on that terrific news later.

But the big difference in the mass-produced Coke and Pepsi versions of bottled water was this. Nothing. It wasn't special water from a special place and, to their credit, the two companies never claimed they were. It tells you right on the Aquafina label, "originates from public water sources." It's kind of small print, but it's there. I'm guessing by now that you know what it means. Tap water. They are selling you tap water in a bottle. Yes, they filter it, but basically you are paying for the same exact shit that you can get by painstakingly turning the handle of your own faucet about half an inch. I know, it's exhausting. It's so much easier to just schlep a forty-two-pound plastic block of forty water bottles from Wal-Mart and then find a spot to put the fucken things. And it is forty-two pounds, I looked it up. The two behemoth companies spent millions of dollars on advertising. Much of the advertising was subtly, and sometimes not so subtly, saying that the water coming out of your tap was contaminated. It wasn't. But thirty-plus years later it has become something of a self-fulfilling prophecy as we have seen in Flint, Michigan, and other places. But basically, they masterfully created what to me is an unlikely but vast market. They convinced presumably normal people to ship, buy, and schlep a product they could already get almost for free almost anywhere. With no schlepping required.

I'm not sure who I owe this quote to, but it's one of my favorites: "When someone shows you who they are, believe them." Pretty simple, right? If someone reveals their true character to you through their words or actions, it's best to accept it and expect it to repeat. A guy who beats the shit out of his wife. She would be wise to acknowledge that he will almost certainly do it again if given the chance. That is who he is, and he has shown her, so she should believe him and get as far away as possible, though we all know it's easy for me to say and much harder than it sounds. What does this have to do with water? Well, to tell you the truth, not much. But sometimes we take shortcuts to *know* what other people *show*. For instance, when I hear anyone blame Biden for inflation, I immediately know that nothing they say can be taken seriously. Because it is impossible. So it throws everything they say into doubt. If they then told me it was raining, I would still have to check. When I see a person who claims to be "liberal" holding a plastic water bottle, I can also dismiss anything else they may say. You cannot hold liberal, environmentalist values and a plastic bottle of water at the same time. Both of these people have shown me exactly who they are. I believe them. See? It was about water after all.

There is no way to overstate the stupidity and horror of single-use plastic water bottles. This subject also could fill its own books. Let's just agree that it is an environmental and public health disaster. A $2.2 trillion disaster as we learned earlier. Just that $2.2 trillion alone would assure a huge chunk of the **Big 4** for everyone. While we are at it, let's all agree that we are idiots to pay for and transport something that is already in your house and office and is nearly free. Even the cheapest filter will make the water out of your tap as good or better than anything sold in a bottle, if it isn't already.

But that dopey shit isn't our only water problem in terms of **4 For All**. Our good friends at the Nestle corporation, along with some hedge funds and private equity firms, are doing their best to buy up water rights across the globe in an attempt to "corner the market and drive-up prices."

Just on the off chance you are thinking that no-one could possibly act this shitty about something so basic to human survival, let me remind you of what Nestle did until they were caught. They used to go into impoverished third-world countries and give away powdered baby formula. They would give away free formula and the fresh water it took to use it. They would continue long enough for the women's natural supply of breast milk to dry up and then stop. Now the family has no choice but to buy the powdered formula from Nestle. Affording it was already a problem. Finding reliable clean water to prepare it was also a huge problem, since Nestle had ceased providing that as well. The result: starving or dead infants. But the story has a happy ending. Nestle had some incredibly profitable years and very happy shareholders. When they were finally held somewhat accountable years later, it cost them much less than they earned killing the kids in the first place. So it all worked out for the best. And of course, no one was ever held criminally responsible.

It's time for us to learn a new economic term: moral hazard. It refers to when a company is incentivized to take risks to **others** that could cause those others serious harm or death but will result in profit for the company. In other words, the consumer gets the risk of death or serious harm, and the company makes a profit. Poor Nestle faced a serious moral hazard when they killed all those kids. Ford faced a similar moral hazard in the 1970s when they killed a whole bunch of people with the Ford Pinto.

The Pinto was one of the first small cars introduced in America after the energy shocks of the early 1970s. It sold a bunch and was pretty cool. It had one small problem: they blew up. If struck from behind, even at slow speeds, a bolt in the fender would pierce the gas tank and produce a quite hearty and satisfying boom! It was really cool to watch, unless you were inside the car and got burned to a crisp, which happened hundreds of times. Court records of Ford internal documents showed that they knew of the problem. They even had devised several cheap and easy fixes and used exactly **none** of them because Ford executives made the calculation and decision that it would be cheaper to pay off the families of the dead than it would be to fix the problem. Again, all of this is proven conclusively in court records of Ford internal documents. I can't make jokes here. This is murder, plain and simple. Not a single Ford executive ever faced a single criminal charge. They were protected by the corporate structure.

These two incidents should be taught over and over again in every school in every country as a cautionary tale of corporate imperialism. It would make all of us much more aware of the amoral, sociopathic nature of corporate behavior. If any individual behaved this way, they would be locked up and the key, quite justifiably, thrown away. In both cases, there were names on those documents. There were **REAL PEOPLE** responsible that we could have identified and held accountable. But we did not. So they quite literally got away with murder. I'm not looking to make any jokes here. The lack of any real consequences for any **individual** in the Ford case changed the world forever. No matter how long I keep yammering on about this, there is just no way to overstate its importance.

Over the years, corporations have been granted almost all of the rights of an individual citizen. What used to be called corruption, throwing handfuls of cash at willing and pliant public servants, is now considered free speech for corporations. What was once called bribery is now just a legal form of corporate free speech. Almost no one can win a public office at any level without some measure of fealty to their corporate donors. A corporate entity now has almost all of the rights of an individual, yet bears none of the **responsibility.** They can buy and sell anyone at any level with impunity. They can overcharge, underserve, and even kill their customers without remorse or consequence.

It's as if we unleashed an army of wealthy, suit-wearing sociopaths upon ourselves. And we have gotten exactly what we deserve. Fucked.

Those two very well-documented events had very real consequences that went well beyond some starving kids and burnt, dead drivers. It made the corporate fortress untouchable, the corporate moat uncrossable. CEOs were made to feel bulletproof because, in very real ways, they are. Understandably it made the boards, Wall Street, and shareholders more demanding of what kind of behavior would be tolerated, even demanded, of the CEOs that made the day-to-day decisions. It's why HMOs red tape their customers literally to death. It's led to millions of corporate decisions that harm their customers and communities with the taxpayer picking up the check.

In a **4 For All** world, we must find a way to pierce the corporate veil. That's a fancy legalese way of simply holding corporate executives responsible for crimes committed by the company. There is no doubt that the failure to hold Ford executives criminally responsible led to deaths caused by other companies. If the United States is to regain its national sovereignty, we must find a way to hold the executives criminally liable when necessary. Doing so would go a long way to incentivize them to avoid those moral hazards. And to hold them to the same standards of behavior as an individual. Nothing less will do.

This seems like the right time to introduce **ALEC**. The lesser-known legacy of the George W. Bush era was the rise of ALEC, The American Legislative Exchange Council. Few people even know of its existence, but it affects your life in a big way. It's the reason your internet sucks dick. It's the reason well-documented mental patients can walk around Wal-Mart with a handgun. Simply put, ALEC is comprised of most of the world's major corporations and billionaires. They literally write laws that they then give to bought-and-owned legislators who pass them, verbatim, often unread.

Obviously, these laws are written to make them even richer and more powerful and have absolutely nothing to do with you, your safety, your survival, or your wellbeing. This may be boring shit, but I assure you that every word of this affects you, is killing many of you, and is turning this once great nation into a third-world country, one fucked-up, self-serving law at a time.

Please accept my apologies. That was some pretty horrifying shit. There was no way to make it fun or cute. It was far too terrible to make light of. So let's move on to education.

17

EDUCATION

Just to lighten the mood for a minute, let's use our imagination again. Imagine a **Big 4** world where every individual gets as much education as they can possibly absorb. Like so many elements of a **Big 4** world, it is difficult to envision just how different it would be.

Every individual would have the opportunity to reach their utmost potential. We would be able to study the things we excel in and enjoy rather than just what we can afford. We would then be able to work in the fields that we **want** to work in rather than fields we might choose because they offer the most security. Because, let's face it, right now virtually every educational decision made is influenced by the need to try to ensure the **Big 4**.

In a perfect world, every person who becomes a doctor would do so out of a profound desire to help the sick. Who becomes a doctor now? Well, first of all, you better be able to afford it. That alone deprives society of most of the people who would take on that responsibility of caring for the sick and dying. So among those that are able to afford it, how many are choosing it just to ensure a life of relatively certain financial security, with no particular altruistic desire? Some? Most? Almost all?

Again, this requires a degree of self-honesty that is difficult for humans. We are even pretty good at convincing ourselves into mindsets we find soothing, or out of those we find uncomfortable. But I'm going to hazard a guess. Half or more of the people who become doctors do it for a reason other than altruism. Maybe they are to trying to begin or continue generational wealth. Maybe they are trying to meet the expectations of somebody else. Who knows? Once again, your guess is every bit as good as mine. But I think we can agree that plenty of people are becoming doctors that just aren't that into those icky sick people. I think we can also agree that there are millions of people out there who would make great doctors if given the opportunity to fulfill their potential. Until we create the **Big 4** world, we will never know.

Unfortunately, we still have to deal with the world as it is right now. And the education world right now is a shit show that is going a long way the wrong way. We could point to the conventional issues of teachers' pay, lack of student achievement, and so on.

The truth is actually more complex, but also simpler, at the same time. Since 1962, the Republican Party has become openly and completely hostile to public education and public educators. That was the year that prayer was officially removed from schools. They also didn't much care for that *Brown v. Board of Education* case in 1954 that brought about school desegregation. Since that day, the Republicans have found any number of ways to destroy public education. They even found one that would create a new pillar of corruption to support their campaigns, kneecap democrats, and sneak Jesus back in all at the same time. Welcome to private (almost always religious) charter schools.

There are times that you have to admire the ingenuity of

evil. This is one of those times. The concept is really simple. As usual, it starts by hijacking public taxpayers' money and funneling it to your friends who then kick some of it back to the politicians to keep the scam going. Our traditional **Triangle Trade of Corruption.**

So the politicians declare that the public schools are failing. They don't mention that they are failing because they themselves underfunded, over-managed, and disrespected them. No, they're just failing because teachers suck, unions suck, and government fucks everything up. Then you propose a "voucher" system. Sounds nice enough, harmless. But what it actually means is that you remove even more dollars from public schools and give taxpayer dollars in the form of vouchers to parents to use at the private charter school of their "choice." That sounds nice. Choice sounds nice. But what it really means is that the parent has a choice of almost always Christian private schools that will enroll their kid for the value of the voucher, which in reality rules out any actual "good" school. Because the "good" schools are exclusive and expensive and certainly wouldn't want any regular (meaning not rich) or, God forbid, black kid from strolling their campus.

So the parent is left with a choice of sub-par religious private schools that make money by the *efficiency* of paying their teachers even less than public schools with no benefits or pesky public teachers unions to deal with. It may also be further away. The parent may have to drive the kid themselves and the education itself might be shitty. But hey, they had a *choice*, right?

I don't want to blow past this "efficiency" argument because it's at the heart of most of the privatization efforts. The argument is that a private entity is always more efficient than government. So you farm out public services to private companies. But their "efficiency" is almost always the same thing. They pay their employees even less than the government did and offer no benefits or job security. They pocket the difference and kick a few bucks back to the corrupt politicians to keep the scam going. Even better, their employees are now paid so little that they qualify for public assistance (welfare) of some sort. So the taxpayer picks up the bill again. I know this is getting repetitive, but there is no way to overstate how much this happens and how much it undermines our society. It's the same shit over and over. Private companies pocketing our tax dollars. All they have to do is grease the politicians.

For the White Republican Christian nationalists, this is a win-win-win situation. You get to hobble one of the last holdouts from union busting. You get kickbacks to your campaign from the new charter school conglomerates that are coagulating as we speak. And you get to sneak Jesus in the back door. Welcome to Republican Heaven.

There's just one small little problem: No one actually gets an education. The charter schools are a joke, underperforming public schools by almost every measure. They are run by people with little to no educational background. They often are not held to the same standards as public schools in terms of background checks and qualifications. It's become the Wild West frontier of education. But at least it's profitable.

Before we move on, I will leave you with but one stat, but an extremely telling and important one.

The average K-12 salary for the 2020-2021 school year for **public school teachers was $64,481.** The average salary for **charter school teachers $48,621.**

It's a single statistic, but it says a lot. That margin reflects the profits to the charter school "industry," the kickbacks for the politicians who keep our taxpayer dollars flowing into private companies, and the poorer quality and vetting of the teachers at the charter schools.

With so-called "school choice" and vouchers, Republicans get everything they always wanted. Decimation of public schools, corrupt political funding from the new charter school industry, further destruction of public unions. And, oh yeah, Jesus back in the schools. Perfection! Unless you actually want to teach anyone anything.

Congratulations! You have successfully navigated the surreal environment of K-12 education in the U.S. with a shiny new high school diploma. It may very well mean you are capable of reading this paragraph. Either way, you now might be ready for college.

18

COLLEGE

At this point you shouldn't be surprised that yet another pillar of corruption stands in your way. Yet another repulsive display of the **Triangle Trade of Corruption.** That is unless you are rich, very prominent on social media, or can dunk a basketball. And the door to this particular shit show was opened by . . . drum roll please . . . ah, fuck it! You have to know by now that it was good old Ronnie Fucken Reagan.

You may have noticed by now that I have a tendency to blame everything on him. But there is good reason. Almost all the elements of the horror show we live through now started with him. But when I say Reagan, I really don't mean Reagan. Because despite photographic evidence to the contrary, there really wasn't a Ronald Reagan. Even before his first campaign for president, he was already displaying symptoms of the Alzheimer's disease that would eventually kill him. By all accounts he was a very nice man and genuinely believed in his own simple, white, closed-minded vision of the world.

He was the perfect stooge to usher in the Powell-memo-inspired corporate vision for America. He was a poor movie actor but an excellent actor within the political realm. A very believable, wise, and folksy uncle. And he would do exactly as instructed by his corporate handlers. It would be wrong to directly blame him for the corporate oligarchy that has enveloped the nation during the last forty-plus years. It would have happened eventually, one way or another. The triumph of the power of money was as inevitable as a leak through a patchwork roof. But he certainly helped paved the way. And for that I lack sufficient moral authority to forgive him. The quality of life for almost every American is worse off for him having existed. Fuck him.

He destroyed students' lives for generations. In place of federally funded scholarships and Pell Grants, there were lenders, both federal and private. He slashed federal spending on higher education by half. As time passed, the states could not bear the additional burden and, by 2020, they too had slashed higher education funding by inflation. Without that funding, higher education costs soared well above the level of inflation. In 1975, the average bachelor graduate left school with $1,000 in debt. By 2020, the average debt was over $37,000. In 1980, the national total of student debt was so small that the number wasn't even tracked. Seriously, I looked for it everywhere. It was negligible. In 2022, student debt has surpassed **$1.75 trillion.**

Student debt is bad news for students. It's also disastrous for the economy overall. The two generations dragging this ball and chain of debt have staggered to start families, to buy homes, or to invest in their own future or retirement. These are the first generations of Americans that **cannot** expect to exceed their parents' financial condition or life expectancy. So when a couple of paragraphs ago I said that he destroyed students' lives, did you think I was exaggerating? I wasn't. This fuck didn't just destroy students, he put a pretty good dent in the whole country.

But as usual, it's even worse than that. Two industries found paradise in the national misery. Lenders and for-profit colleges thrived. In many cases, the lenders paired up with the for-profit colleges to fleece the most vulnerable, especially low-income and minority would-be students. The colleges created vast marketing and sales schemes to lure in students and then left them saddled in high-interest debt. Here is my favorite part. In the forty-plus years since Reagan set out to destroy higher learning, Congress has acted five times on behalf of the lenders. By 2005, it became almost impossible to discharge student loan debt, even through bankruptcy. These victims are victims for life.

Is it in view yet? The triangle, can you see it? Just in case you can't, the banks and for-profit colleges make absurd amounts of money. They kick some of it back to the politicians to keep the scam going. It's the same exact **Triangle Trade of Corruption** at work. Many—not all, but many—of these for-profit colleges are complete scams. It's safe to say all are at least somewhat scammy. Most spend more on marketing and sales than on all things educational. Some just vanish, leaving students drowning in debt and not even with the degree that is usually close to worthless anyway. You've all seen the commercials. Just try to imagine that any real institution of higher learning would even **need** to advertise.

But the lenders and shit-bag colleges have become yet another pillar in the structure of corruption, providing reliable campaign contributions for the pliable. It's OK. It's normal for a society to sacrifice its children so that a few people profit and a few win re-election. We don't mind that our kids literally get shot for profit. Why should we mind if the survivors get financially raped as well? With that rape continuing for their entire financial life. We'll talk about how to fix this shit later. In the meantime, let's get the fuck out of here. It stinks. And besides, it's time for a completely incongruent musing.

19

LOVE

LOVE STORIES ARE WRITTEN AND LIVED BY THE SECURE

Let's avoid for the moment that the above sentiment is not completely true. But if you give it some thought, as I have, you might conclude, again as I have, that love is a lot easier when you are not starving to death. I believe in true romantic love. It's on the short list of things worth living for. But what is love in a world where basic survival is always the first order of business? First on the to-do list, the very history of love, marriage, and partnership is transactional in nature. Until fairly recently, love wasn't even part of the equation of marriage and child rearing. And I think we would be lying to ourselves if we didn't admit that even now a man's wallet and earning potential plays an outsized role in determining his desirability as a mate. And if that paints women as superficial, it would still pale when compared to the breathtaking male superficiality when it comes to choosing a mate.

The point, if indeed there is one, is that "true" romantic love may well flourish in a **4 For All** world. Our greatest romantic literature features characters that are free of fear of financial ruin and homelessness. Few such works are written involving people working three part-time jobs just to avoid eviction. One such novel, *Romance on the Curb* shows love flourish among personal belongings strewn on the street as a ruggedly handsome sheriff's deputy serves an eviction notice to a blushing, love-struck newly homeless woman. It's every bit as romantic as it is completely made up.

Which leads me to my last question before we get back to work: Is romantic love transactional by nature? In a **4 For All** world, we would get to find out. So let's talk food.

20

FOOD

There is a ton of good news here. Really, there is. Of course, there is plenty of corporate fuckery as well. Maybe even more than in some of the other subjects we have discussed. The **Triangle Trade of Corruption** is particularly well fed in this industry. It's not necessary to pardon the awful pun.

But first, some really good news: **lab-grown meat**. It's coming, and faster than anyone could have anticipated. It won't be long before we can buy any kind of meat that we buy now but that comes completely from cells grown in a laboratory. I know. It feels a little creepy. But it is really important that we get over that little bit of creepiness because the rewards of lab-grown meat for you and society at large are nothing short of world changing and miraculous. First of all, there would be no more factory farms. The end of this disgusting cruelty alone is more than enough reason to just shut up and eat the lab-grown meat. And trust me, you won't be able to tell the difference. It will seem identical because it *is* identical. Here are just some of the reasons it's such a big deal:

- **ANTIBIOTICS** – As we talked about earlier, factory farms use more than 160 billion tons of antibiotics each year. Every study shows it is a major contributing factor to antibiotic resistance in humans. And the development of antibiotic-resistant bacteria. The so-called superbugs and even scarier untreatable bugs.

- **WASTE** – Poo-poo and pee-pee from factory farms put us all neck deep in environmental caca. I apologize for my use of such technical terms, but since we're on the subject, let's talk farts. Cow and sheep farts more specifically. According to real data, 14.5 percent of human-induced global greenhouse gas emissions come from livestock, which would be hysterical if it weren't terrifying.

- **FEED** – This actually is kind of technical. The food we feed farm animals is inefficient, meaning the world would have more food by not passing it first through the animal on its way to the slaughterhouse. Data on this varies a lot. But the least terrible numbers I found say that we lose caloric value at a 3-to-1 ratio. That means we get three times as many calories by just eating the feed rather than feeding it to a doomed animal and then eating him or her. Author's note: I don't think animals on their way to the slaughterhouse are particularly concerned about pronouns.

- **ENVIRONMENTAL IMPACT** – Animal agriculture is associated with significant environmental challenges, including deforestation, greenhouse gas emissions, water pollution, and biodiversity loss. Those are just words on a page, but the real-life impacts are all too real. For instance, thirty-four percent of all global cropland is used to produce animal feed. That's just their feed and doesn't count the land used for the animals themselves. Another twenty-six percent—in other words, more than half of the earth's dry surface—is being used to make meat. That's fucken insane. I kept checking those stats over and over because I couldn't believe it's real. But it is.

- **DEFORESTATION** – Huge swaths of area are basically leveled to farm livestock. The losses from this alone are massive and include loss of human habitats, animal habitats, and diversion and use of enormous amounts of water. It also compounds global warming and greenhouse gases in the atmosphere.

I'm really just scratching the surface here. The costs to all of us for meat consumption and livestock farming, factory or otherwise, are so vast that it's difficult to fully comprehend the scope of how disastrous it is. Both for the planet and ourselves.

But look, I'm not telling you it's immoral to eat meat or that you should stop. I like meat. I eat it. Sometimes I don't feel that great about it, but this is one of those times that there really is a happy ending without my customary obnoxious sarcasm. Lab-grown meat is coming, and soon. And it won't be all that long before it's the same price or cheaper than what you are buying now. Even better, it won't be chock full of antibiotics, hormones, or other crap. It will be as clean and healthy as meat can possibly be. In fact, there will be some varieties that are downright healthy by even the most stringent dietary standards.

By now you are probably looking over your shoulder to see how the **Triangle Trade of Corruption** might screw this up. It's a valid concern considering that only five companies control almost all meat production in the U.S. Maybe they just decide to smother the lab-grown industry in its cradle. Something Big Oil has done to emerging technology more times than I can count over the last century. But in this instance, I'm not worried. The big boys seem to have taken the "let's own it" philosophy rather than the "let's kill it" philosophy. So it's coming, and it can't get here fast enough for my taste (pardon the pun).

Let's go off topic for a moment. The tobacco industry faced a similar dilemma not too long ago when vaping started growing in popularity. There was about a five-year stretch where you could observe the tobacco industry trying to make up their mind whether to *own* it or *kill* it. They ended up doing a bit of both, a hybrid strategy. On one hand they bought up some of the better known and consolidated vape brands. At the same time, they used their political power over the FDA (see regulatory capture) to start muddying the waters and producing studies conflating the dangers of vaping with the dangers of smoking. They even went so far as to have our old friend **ALEC** push through state laws to ban vaping and to treat it the same way as cigarette smoking, making it illegal to vape in public the same way it was illegal to smoke. They succeeded spectacularly. In the public consciousness, vaping is considered as deadly as smoking and subject to the same, if not harsher restrictions.

I'm not here to defend either smoking or vaping, but the argument that they are equally harmful is about the same as saying that burning your finger on a hot pan is the same as burning down your house with you in it. I'm not saying vaping is good for you. The only thing that is a hundred percent safe to put in your lungs is air. But cigarettes contain a couple hundred dangerous and/or carcinogenic substances. Vapes have zero, or one, depending whose studies you read. Not the same. Not even close.

OK, back to food. There is even more genuinely great news.

We can easily produce enough food for everyone. Even more so once lab-grown meat is brought to scale. And even accounting for the inevitable effects of climate change, we're in good shape. But I would be remiss if I didn't at least touch on some of the problems brought on by our reining corporate oligarchy. The first one has its roots in the very early days of the Powell Memorandum and its blueprint for private domination of the public realm:

- **Dairy** – First off, has it ever occurred to you how weird it is to drink and otherwise consume the milk of a different species? Humans and our pets are almost the only ones on the planet that do it. It **is** weird, and it can almost be said to be unnatural. Why? Because sixty-five percent of humans are lactose intolerant, meaning they lack an enzyme that breaks down the lactose in all dairy products. Another three percent or so have an allergy to dairy, so it would be reasonable to question how dairy became a staple of our diets and so ubiquitous despite the fact that less than a third of people can eat it without clearing out a room full of people and making long-term reservations on the toilet. It's clearly bad for us. I could cite a thousand studies and prove to you dozens of different ways that it is bad for us. All this while delivering only the most marginal nutritional rewards. And most of that is artificially added anyway, like the vitamin D added to milk. Milk, probably brought to you in a plastic bottle which you might as well eat, since it's ending up in our bodies anyway. A history of dairy in the U.S. is a history of the early days of regulatory capture. Going back to that very first Food Pyramid from the FDA. Look, I love ice cream and butter even though they make me sick. But don't try to tell me that dairy is good for us. "Only don't tell me that you're innocent. Because it insults my intelligence, and it makes me very angry." Sorry, that was Michael Corleone. Oh, just in case you weren't already disgusted, we, the taxpayers, actually give the industry hundreds of millions of dollars in direct subsidies. Money straight from us fat, diabetic, high-cholesterol taxpayers.

- **Sugar/corn syrup** – Oy. If you hated that bit about dairy, this one will make you plotz. First of all, the numbers. We the people pay, through subsidies, more than $4 billion a year to this industry. Yes, the industry that makes us fat and diabetic. Yes, the industry that costs us hundreds of billions in healthcare dollars. Yes, the industry that causes premature death and disability to millions. Yes, the industry that secures and assures diabetics for Big Pharma to treat with ridiculously overpriced insulin and other very expensive medical interventions. I'm going to create my own economic term for this form of collaboration: **repulsive symbiosis.** The sugar folks provide the pharma folks with millions of victims to "treat" and make billions. And the taxpayer picks up the tab. If you have reached this point of the book and you still believe that our current economic system is capitalism, then I am a truly terrible writer, or you are a "slow adult," a permissible term that substitutes for the more descriptive but not permissible "retard." And calling you a retard is an insult to retards. They are blameless. You are intentionally stupid. And it gets even worse. Production of both corn for corn syrup and sugar are disastrous environmentally and waste and foul an enormous amount of water. If you are going to subsidize something with taxpayer money, why not pay for things that don't suck.

- **Wheat/soybeans/rice** – Between the three, the taxpayer kicks in a few billion a year through a combination of subsidies, tariffs, and price controls. I didn't go crazy researching on this, and I'm sure there are some shenanigans at play, but for the most part this area seems to make sense. The taxpayer via the federal government has some place in keeping the price of consumer staples stable. I get it, and more or less agree with it. However, you must know that these policies are way more socialism than they are free market capitalism. So perhaps it's a good time to consider the -ism as less relevant than the result.

- **Almonds** – I couldn't quite leave the food section without pissing off liberal hipsters. Almond milk is not "milk." I can't even figure out why you would want it to be. Hey, maybe you like almonds. Maybe you like almond "milk." That's fine, just don't fool yourself. Almonds are no bargain environmentally, nutritionally, or even financially. Almond farming is in some ways even worse than dairy farming in terms of land and water use and pollution. On the other hand, almonds don't cry when you pull on their tits.

21

———————

CLOTHING

To me, this is one of the more interesting parts of the **Big 4**. Clothing is incredibly cheap to produce in volume. Almost all of its final price to the consumer is affected in ways different than most other consumer goods. Style has never been my strong suit. I tend to keep things simple, mostly out of a desire to not embarrass myself any more than necessary. "Clothes make the man" is an age-old truth. I walk into a supermarket dressed in my work clothing, which is a full suit and tie, and the seas part. It's not my imagination that I'm treated with respect that verges on deference. But you take the same schlep (me) in my occasional shorts and V-neck T-shirt and might as well be a different person. People avoid direct eye contact and often pelt me with partially rotten fruit. OK, the difference isn't that huge, but it's most definitely real.

I doubt that it's an exaggeration to say that hundreds if not thousands of books have been written on the subject of clothing and style and its place in society. But I know it's powerful and I can prove it with a single example. Many otherwise rational people will think nothing of paying $1,000 for a Coach purse that has the exact same utility as a Wal-Mart or

Amazon purse of the same size that costs about $10. Yes, of course the Coach purse will last a bit longer than the ten-dollar purse, but I think it's safe to say it won't last a hundred times longer. Not to mention that the Coach purse may go out of style in a year or two and be sidelined by the very thing that made it worth a grand to someone in the first place.

Another thing about expensive style accessories, this time on the men's side. And for this I will use a story from my own life. I became fascinated with the idea of owning a Rolex. The one I wanted was about $8,000 at the time—a stainless steel, blue and gold Sub-Mariner. I finally cruised to St. Thomas and got one. A little cheaper than in the states but still about $8,000. My wife at the time, a gambling drug addict, stole it. Not once, but twice. Both times pawning it for whatever they would give her so that she could continue gambling or drugging or whatever the fuck she was doing. On both occasions, she alerted me the day before the pawn shop would declare her in default and "keep" the watch. Both times, genius that I am, I rushed to the pawn shop and paid the ransom. A couple thousand dollars each time. In case you're wondering, I don't blame her at all for the second time she stole it, only the first. I sold the watch not long after I got it back the second time.

Yes, I know I mentioned those incidents earlier and I'm getting a bit off subject here for a change, but I learned a valuable lesson from this experience. I no longer own ANYTHING that will break my heart if I lose it. There are exceptions. Family photos, a very small number of keepsakes, and the like. But nothing anyone has any financial incentive to steal. If you were to come to my goofy little apartment right now, the combined resale value of EVERYTHING in it is less than a couple grand. It includes two really nice TVs, a decent tablet, a laptop, and some distinctively and aggressively unstylish clothing. That's it! Go ahead, take it. I'll send you my address. I could replace the things I need with one paycheck. I learned this lesson from a repulsive, dog-murdering, narcissistic sociopath who was almost certainly a schizophrenic. I take no pleasure in that precise description, but it serves as a reminder that we can learn something from everyone and everything.

Let's get back to clothes. The very existence of Rolex and Coach shows us that clothes and accessories are about a lot more than clothes and accessories. There's social status, virtue signaling, and social belonging, but one thing I haven't found much of in the fashion world is the **Triangle Trade of Corruption**. There's some good stuff:

- **Confidence** – Being well dressed can lend a person pride and confidence. Keyword there being *lend*.
- **Cultural and Historical Significance** – It can build and maintain social and cultural bonds.
- **Import Industry and Jobs** – It plays a role in the economy and employment.
- **Trends and Innovation** – There are times when fashion trends seem silly to those of us outside of that world. But there is no doubt that a great deal of skill and artistry goes into the design and creation of clothing and accessories. It's clearly an art form.

Unfortunately, just like everything else, there's a fair amount of poop:

- **Marketing and Manipulation** – They create a demand. They create a perceived value. And it causes some financial distress for those who couldn't and shouldn't afford to try and keep up.
- **Labor Practices** – Let's just say that some of the most expensive things in the world are made by some of the lowest-paid people in the world.

- **Body Image and Unrealistic Expectations** – The fashion industry has always been the front line of creating and profiting from an absurd standard of beauty that almost no one can possibly live up to. And men are nowhere near man enough to do anything but to accept that standard for the women they find attractive. This is no one's "fault" in particular, it just is. All of our standards have been warped and are impossibly high. Because the Barbie dolls men have been brainwashed to seek simply do not exist outside the toy store. In a way it comes down to a joke nearly a century old. Groucho Marx said, "I don't want to belong to any club that would have me as a member." The fashion and cosmetics industries are just as good as anyone to blame.
- **Fast Fashion and Planned Obsolescence** – This has led to a world literally smothered in clothing. Full closets, full drawers, full storage units and eventually full cargo ships carrying the excess of the first world to the third world. Which we would initially think is a good thing. But then there's that fucken law of *unintended consequences*. Even when our intentions are good.
- **Disruption of Local Textile Industry** – Jobs are lost and factories shuttered in the places that can least afford it. And even smaller, artisan operations are decimated in the face of massive deposits of free or almost free clothes.
- **Dependency and Loss of Self-Sufficiency** – Constant reliance on donated clothing can create a dependency mindset and discourage local production and self-sufficiency. Instead of investing in local manufacturing and development of textile industries, communities may come to rely solely on

external donations, which can hinder long-term economic growth and self-reliance.

- **Environmental Impact** – The donation of surplus clothing can contribute to environmental problems in recipient countries. The discarded clothing that cannot be sold or used often ends up in landfills, adding to waste management challenges. Additionally, the production and transportation of donated clothing have their own environmental impacts, including carbon emissions and water consumption. The water part was particularly disturbing and, even after checking numerous sources, I can still barely believe it. Apparently it takes about seven hundred gallons of water to make a single cotton T-shirt. Yeah, figure that shit out.
- **Cultural Displacement** – Western clothing donations can influence and displace local traditional dress and cultural identities. When traditional attire is replaced by donated clothing, it can erode cultural diversity and disrupt social and cultural practices that are deeply rooted in communities.

Despite all the issues we see above, we really are in great shape when it comes to clothing. I'm completely making this up, but I suspect we could stop manufacturing clothing altogether for two decades and we would still have enough for everyone to be properly, if not stylishly, clothed. Almost nothing would need to change to bring about this part of the **Big 4** world that we will soon be fighting for. But for now, let's talk about a bunch of seemingly random things under the general heading of Capitalism.

22

CAPITALISM

THE BIG OX THAT COULD

If you have come this far, you are probably not quite sure what to make of me politically speaking. If you are what passes for "conservative" in this day and age, you would have already dismissed me as some kind of a commie and tossed this book in the trash quite some time ago, probably pushing it under some other garbage just to make sure that no one else finds it and becomes infected.

But if you're still here, you may have good reason to wonder. So this is as good a time as any to confess to the crime of narcissism. I think anyone who writes, performs, acts, does stand-up, etc., almost certainly has some narcissistic traits. It's a must. In my case particularly so because I specifically constructed this book to have a conversational tone. But only in tone. Because I'm doing all the talking and the only way you can interrupt me is to stop reading. So my motivation, aside from saving the world, is to be heard. It is undoubtedly a form of attention-seeking behavior. The truth is I just want to be heard and read. I genuinely don't care about money. I say "genuinely" because most often when someone says it's not about the money, it's almost always about the money. Not this time. No, I'm not rich but I'm just fine without earning a penny from writing. Which is good because, believe me, I'm not making any. Which also does drive home the point that money only really matters when you don't have any. Having a ton of money will buy you the opportunity for happiness, but not the happiness itself. Having no money matters a great deal. Money then becomes the **only** thing that matters. What a billionaire pays for parking is an existential amount of money to the ninety-nine percent. It is literally a matter of life and death. The stakes are that high.

The thing about the **Big 4** world we are going to make is that it lowers those stakes for everyone. With our basic survival assured, there just won't be that many make or break, life or death decisions, financial or otherwise. Imagine that all of us are seated at a humongous poker table. Right now, we know that if we have a little run of bad cards or bad luck we can end up broke and busted. In a **4 For All** world the stakes of that game would be much lower and the results less stressful.

But getting back to attention-seeking behavior. I've already admitted my own, so forgive me or don't. Your call. But have you noticed a drastic increase in attention-seeking behavior in general? I perceive a wave of attention-seeking behavior that seemingly coincided with the 2016 election of that portly orange fellow. Say or think whatever you want about the guy, but there are a couple of things about him that are undoubtedly true.

Getting attention is the only thing he really cares about. If he became the lifelong dictator of the United States as many believe was and is his goal, even that would still only be a means to the end of getting and maintaining attention. It's as if he is locked in as a lifelong teenager desperately trying to get the attention of his parents. And to keep getting attention, you have to keep topping yourself. You have to be ever more reckless, ever more daring, and ever crazier. The thing is though, it's contagious. I don't want to blame everything on him because there's already dozens of documented reasons that prove he's basically just a fat, repulsive, born-rich nitwit. But he does have a gift. He instinctively knows how to get and keep getting attention. Society has become louder, ruder, and stupider in part because he has made it OK to say or do anything. To lie, cheat, steal, and corrupt without consequence.

But there are consequences for the rest of us that go way beyond politics and economics. There is an epidemic of loneliness in this country at the same time that's it's never been easier to "reach out and touch someone." In study after study, they are finding that "estrangement" is rampant in our society. Families and friends are writing each other out of their lives in record numbers. We have all built walls to keep out the noise, but the result is that we are estranging our loved ones with all of our new "boundaries."

Social media is right there to give you a quick and completely wrong answer to any social situation you might face. The result is millions of parents estranged from their kids, more than at any other time in our history. At a time where we need our loved ones the most, we are losing them over the smallest of slights. Crossing someone's boundary can be as simple as telling them something they just don't want to hear. Of course, no one should subject themselves to abuse, be it physical, emotional, or sexual. Some lines should never be crossed and certainly not be allowed to be crossed a second time.

But the truth is that if you know ANYONE long enough, they will eventually do something to piss you off or vice versa. Much like the idea that personal freedom necessitates a certain amount of personal responsibility. I think that we all might be better off if we remember to balance our boundaries with an equal measure of understanding and forgiveness. Give extra thought to exactly where you place those boundaries. If your aunt tells you that your Thanksgiving stuffing sucks, you don't have to write her out of your life forever. And you might want to consider that your stuffing might genuinely suck. It did seem kind of dry.

But back to our fat orange friend. I contend that he is the result of our corruption and decay. Not the cause. Republicans since Nixon had already been slowly losing touch with reality. It's as if the entire Republican Party suffered from Reagan's Alzheimer's. For four decades they have been saying and doing crazier and crazier things and moving further and further to the right. I feel safe in saying that Reagan himself couldn't run as a Republican in the 2020s. The 1956 Republican platform resembles the 2020 Democratic platform. In 2020, the Republicans didn't even bother to create a platform. Trump was the result of this degeneration, not the cause. He was the first to understand that he could say absolutely ANYTHING, as long as he said it loud and often. And we are all Trump. Living in a world of constant noise and sensory overload. Social media was supposed to give all of us a voice. And we have used that voice to call strangers "fuckface" on Instagram. We are all drowning in noise. This may be a case of "you kids get off my lawn," but has anyone noticed that popular music contains a lot more screaming? No, I'm not ruminating about the good old days and saying that new music is shit, but it does really seem like there is a lot more yelling in popular music these days. Just more examples of more people ever more desperate to be heard. It even seems as if people speak louder than they used to. And I don't think it's just me. I'm getting old, I'm supposed to hear *less*.

And lies. Remember Steve Bannon? Remember "Flood the zone with shit"? It works. There is no longer even an objective reality for us to rely on. The result is that we have never been louder, and we have never had less to say. Everyone is loud, angry, and adrift in a sea of uncertainty. Most of us are getting poorer, sicker, and less secure than any generation since The

Great Depression. We are pissed off. And for most of us, we have good reason but no idea who to blame. So we round up the usual suspects. Black folks are always convenient. Immigrants are always trying to take your job. Anybody gay or transgender is probably up to no good. Lately, the MAGA folks are really obsessed with all things gay or transgender. The governor of Florida even picked a fight with Mickey Mouse and drag queens. It's weird, even for them. Something tells me that Governor DeSantis doth protest too much, if you catch my drift.

Jews are always pretty reliable to get a certain crowd worked up too. But what they are really mad at is capitalism. Or more to the point, the lack of any genuine capitalism. You had to figure I would work my way around to it eventually.

Capitalism is the worst economic system ever created. Its only virtue is that it's better than every other choice. And it's true. There is a reason that economics is called "The Dismal Science." It's because it always has to take into account the worst of basic human instincts. Every expert on the financial markets will tell you that it is fear and greed that move markets. Add envy and stupidity and you have the basis of economics.

But the reality is that I am a firm believer in capitalism and free markets. But it is not a magic wand. I figure that capitalism does the best job of channeling some of our worst instincts into positive results. Think of it this way, capitalism is the most powerful and wonderful beast of burden imaginable. It is an ox that, when *properly yoked*, will till our fields perfectly and quickly and provide abundance for us all. Notice the "properly yoked" part. As wonderful as this animal is, if not properly harnessed, it will shit all over everyone and eat our children. That is where we are now. The animal that is capitalism has broken free of its bonds and runs roughshod over our people, governments, freedom, and democracy. There must be some rules that ensure a fair playing field and which trim the excesses. The problem is, as I've been babbling on relentlessly, that the players are now so big that they can push the referees around at will, which is yet another way of saying "regulatory capture."

The problem from a public policy standpoint is that we are now mostly idiots. We no longer seem capable of having any form of real or nuanced discussion of issues. The right calls every regulation or social program "socialism," and the left calls every capitalist a greedy money grubber. Yes, that's an over-simplification, but I think it's a fair one and gets the point across.

Capitalism is very, very good at some things. And as we have seen already, it is very, very bad at others. The trick is to stop thinking in terms of "-isms" (which most people don't understand anyway) and take an honest look at what works and what doesn't. Republicans have spent forty-plus years telling everyone that government sucks at everything. Then they get themselves elected and prove it.

Honestly, how do you run on a policy of being anti-government and then actually govern? The answer is no, you don't. Somebody, somewhere tell me something Republicans are in favor of. We only know what they hate. Government, gays, immigrants. Do me a favor, please! Build a bridge somewhere or a road, or a school, or some fucken thing. They gave out almost $5 trillion in tax cuts when they held office and then resisted spending even one dime on infrastructure to benefit the American people once they were out. We are a laughable, wobbly, crumbling country, teetering on the edge of genuine third-world status and we don't even notice.

And as far down as we have gone, we can still fix it. All it takes is one honest conversation. What things should government do? What things should be public sector? That's it! It's as easy to say as it is seemingly impossible to do, because the zone is flooded with shit. But it is really the only political question you need to ask. I'm not completely dismissing the importance of the "hot button" issues that both sides are constantly pushing. Social issues are important. Gun rights and/or control is important. Abortion rights are important, as are civil rights for everyone. And everyone means EVERYONE.

Sidetrack notice: One issue that makes everyone crazy can be fixed in five minutes. But it won't be. Why? Because oligarchs like slaves. Yes, I'm talking about immigration.

23

IMMIGRATION

Most Republicans are racist and object to non-white immigrants for reasons that are completely based in white supremacy. Yeah, I went there. But is that true? I don't know, you tell me, is it? Yeah, I think so. Democrats attack them for it, but it doesn't work because Republicans fully understand their base. And more importantly they understand the raw power of fear as a motivational force. Thus, the nonsense that is "The Great Replacement" theory. Because at heart, white people like me fear the loss of the total dominance of everything that they have enjoyed for a thousand years. And worse, what if a new, non-white majority treats whites the way **they were treated** for that same thousand years. Uh-oh. I look back at these last few sentences and think "holy shit, that's hardcore." The trouble is, unfortunately, I'm probably quite horribly right. Assata, that was for you.

Well, I'm going to pretend I didn't say any of that out loud and move on. We will always have illegal immigrants and illegal workers because illegal workers are the next best thing to slaves. And the corporations want the cheapest labor they can get. And since they own the government, both parties will yell about the issue, but they will never actually address it.

Before we go on, I need to make clear that I am not against immigration. We are all immigrants, and we need immigrants. And they actually pay way more into our economy than they could ever hope to take out. I know. You've been lied to and told they are a drain on social services. It's the exact opposite. And even though I am pro-immigrant, illegal workers are a huge problem for ALL workers for exactly the reason our corporate overlords insist on having them. They lower ALL wages.

Think about it. If you can pay someone $2 an hour to stand up to their necks in chicken guts or worse, care for your parents, why not? And even better, they can't complain about it lest someone calls the INS and the next stop is Guatemala. Even if they aren't from Guatemala. I made that part up. I just felt like saying Guatemala. It sounds so, you know, foreign.

But for real, cheap labor that can't complain or receive any benefits is very, very good for business. If you had to pay them the true market value of that labor, we can make a reasonable guestimate. Take the roughly fourteen million illegal workers out of the economy and there would be no argument for a minimum wage. We wouldn't need it.

Let's take a brief but important detour to remind you of one HUGE THING. You pay Wal-Mart workers even if you never buy a thing from them. The same is true of every fast-food restaurant and Amazon and hundreds of other employers. More than four million people work for Wal-Mart and Amazon. A vast majority of their employees qualify for "welfare" of some form. It is estimated that the taxpayer kicks in somewhere between $5 and $8 per hour for every Amazon, Wal-Mart, and fast-food employee. So you might as well shop there. You might as well eat their garbage. Because you already virtually eat their shit.

Let me walk you through this because it may not be so

obvious to you as it is to me. They pay their employees starvation wages. The taxpayer pays the difference (that $5 to $8 per hour), just enough to keep their employees from starving to death and keep them showing up for work. The companies make billions in profits. The taxpayers pay out billions in benefits to the workers, so it is precisely as if YOU/WE are paying their labor costs while the company makes the profit. Again, this is the exact opposite of free market capitalism and yet another example of the **Triangle Trade of Corruption.**

If your business plan involves and depends on the taxpayer paying your employees, then you don't have a business plan. You have a **corporate welfare** plan. And because of corruption, because they own the government, it works. In a real free market capitalist democracy, no business would be considered viable if it depended on taxpayer dollars to exist. The corollary to this, of course, is that any person who is fully employed should be paid sufficiently to survive without the need for public assistance. So let's move on and see how removing slave labor from the labor pool would practically eliminate this immense flow of corporate welfare.

Once illegal immigrant workers are removed from the labor pool, we would have a genuine "free market" of labor. At that point, even the cheapest labor would cost you about $14 an hour. That's the bottom rung and the lowest of all the estimates I found. And everything up the ladder would rise accordingly. Picking apples would pay $14, McDonald's would have to pay seventeen or more, and so on. Would some things cost more? Sure. They would cost what they really cost without being subsidized by illegal labor and artificially suppressed wages that go with it. That's what a free market does when it's actually free and not artificially distorted by near-slave labor.

"But it's impossible," I hear you thinking. "How do you stop illegal immigration?" you ask. Look, I'm an idiot and I figured it out in two minutes. A MILLION DOLLAR FINE FOR **HIRING**

AN ILLEGAL IMMIGRANT. Fines then double for companies or individuals that keep offending, and at the end you tuck in a couple potential criminal charges for large-scale offenses and offenders. I know the criminal charges are near impossible at the moment. We've already seen corporations literally murder people without consequence. But stay with me here. We can change that.

And that would be it! It's over. By doing that, you remove the financial incentive for both the employer and the illegal worker. No employer would dare chance it because it isn't financially worth the risk. And no one would sneak in here if there was no possibility of getting a job. That's not one hundred percent true. Not every illegal immigrant is here for a job. But it's an overwhelming percentage. And since there would not be a lot of people trying to sneak in, you can really focus our existing resources on drug cartels and terrorists.

At that point you can begin to have a rational conversation about how much immigration the country wants and needs. The truth is we would need quite a bit for our aging population and declining birthrates. We could once again become the country where every smart person around the world wants in. From what I could tell, the net numbers wouldn't end up that different.

The benefits to our country would be too many to count. Some prices would rise while others would fall. Money spent on immigration prevention can be reallocated to prevent more serious dangers. People will have a lot more money to spend and the government would collect a lot more revenue to spend on stupid things like roads, bridges, electrical grids, water systems, and shoring up the country against the changes of global warming. It's a win-win-win for everybody, even the immigrants. They would no longer have to try dangerous and expensive attempts to cross the border. And once they are here, they can work safely and fully participate in their communities and economy. Once you sort it all out, the net immigration number probably wouldn't change much. The only real difference would be a safer, richer country.

So there we have a simple and effective fix for a seemingly intractable problem, much like the **Big 4** itself. We have to **choose** to do it. Again, I am not naïve. Obnoxious, but not naïve. Our corporate masters will not be so eager to give up nearly free labor. But the irony here is that, in the long run, it would probably benefit them as well. They would have access to a larger pool of legal labor, much of it educated and all of it very motivated. And they would have the pricing power to pass along some of those extra expenses to a consumer who just so happens to have more money to spend.

Would this plan cause some short-term disruption? Sure. But I'd bet that it gets sorted out pretty quickly and the country gains a new and much better "normal." It's amazing how much closer we can get to a **Big 4** world just by fixing this one, ridiculously fixable problem. But now let's get back to our furry friend.

24

CAPITALISM

THE BIG OX THAT COULD (PART 2)

A rational conversation would be a matter of deciding which things should be done as part of the public sector (government) and which things should be part of the private sector (free market). I am aware that, at the moment, no such conversation is possible. Many people are ignorant, and many have been deliberately lied to and misled, their zones flooded with shit. Also, as we know, our government does not actually work for us. They work for their corporate owners.

We know that the government is still pretty good at doing the things it wants to do, what it prioritizes. It is still effective in the areas that it prioritizes. The problem is that for now, the priority is never the American people and our needs. They prioritize the needs of the corporations and billionaires that keep them in office. Occasionally they bow to the whim of fat, angry white people who have suddenly become deathly afraid of drag queens and Bud Light. The same people can also kick politicians out of public life at their whim by backing a different candidate. Politicians know they must toe that line if they want to keep their jobs.

All these things and more make it impossible to have such a

conversation. But to get to a **Big 4** world we must have it and so we will. We will get into the how part later. But for now, let's just sort it all out. We've already discussed that, in general, the free market is best for **most** things we **want**. Public ownership is preferable for the things we **need.**

To me there is a pretty simple litmus test, and it comes in question form. How much would you pay for water? If you don't have any water, the answer would be anything, everything. You would give everything if your alternative were dying of thirst. To me that's a pretty good place to draw the line between public and private. If a private company controlled your only source of water, they could charge $1 million a bottle. And don't laugh, it's going in that direction. Private companies are buying up municipal sources and other water supplies with that exact hope. Build a monopoly or a semi-monopoly of water. You've seen how well that works for electric service. So basically, that is my argument for separation of public versus free market. If it is something that will kill you if you don't get it, then it is best if we the people own and operate it as part of a democracy. The owners are us, and we answer to us through our democratically elected officials.

I know that last line looks like a cruel joke. Because, right now, our democracy is run by money and corporations. It has also been hobbled by decades of underfunding, neglect, and decay to the point that you wouldn't be wrong in saying that our democracy and government is pretty close to useless. The result of yet another self-fulfilling prophecy. Demonize something long enough, you create for yourself a genuine demon.

But it wasn't always that way and it doesn't have to be that way. That is why the Republican obsession with hatred of government is so pernicious. Because when you say government is bad, what are you really saying? Remember that in a democracy the government is supposed to be a reflection of its people. So when you say a democratically elected government is bad, you are saying "We the People" are bad. Honestly, can you think of a less patriotic thing to say or believe? These fucks that wrap themselves in the flag and wear it on their lapel are the least patriotic people imaginable. If you believe in America, then you must believe in its people. So, are we the people bad? I don't think so, and at this point it doesn't even matter because we don't really have a say in things anyway. Money and power control us and our elections. We can fix that. And we will. And once that happens, I think we will find out that we agree way more than we disagree and that we really aren't that bad. Whenever you think of government, think of it as **being us.** Because it is, or at least it's supposed to be. And it will be again.

So if we want the government (us) to run the things that will kill us if we don't have them, then the dividing line becomes surprisingly clear. It's most, but not all, of the **Big 4/7:**

- **Water**
- **Healthcare** – As discussed above. For-profit medicine simply doesn't work. A single payer *Medicare for all* like system certainly would work and would also make healthcare much cheaper overall. Some of the same businesses that oppose it would end up benefiting from it. Consider this, Ford makes cars. OK, some of them used to blow up and kill people. But I say forgive and forget (not really). But they very much want to be in the car business. Wal-Mart wants to be in the selling cheap plastic crap business. My company wants to be in the casino business. But the insanity of it all is that all of us are forced to be in the business of healthcare. It costs us a fortune just to even try and do right by our employees and offer them some form of coverage. We spend a small, but actually huge, fortune just to offer them anything. And it's all crap because all of

the insurance "products" are crap. It costs us a fortune and requires many of us to employ armies of HR people to administer this garbage. I bet my boss and a million other bosses would be absolutely thrilled to be out of the healthcare business. I get the giggles when I see commercials for HMOs that tell me how I can buy a healthcare plan tailored to my needs. What the fuck does that even mean? How could anyone know in advance what they need? We are supposed to decide what to cover and what not to cover? Unless I'm crazy and/or clairvoyant, how in the world can I know which things I need covered? How about this? If and when I get sick I would like healthcare. Oops, I guessed wrong, and it turns out I only covered my left nut for testicular cancer and it's in my right nut. Tough luck. I'm not covered. Please accept my most sincere apologies for the disturbing optic. But now I find myself wondering if it is possible to switch your nuts around. I've never tried it, and I am explicitly telling any reader with testicles **not** to try it. Can you imagine that lawsuit? Tease alert: I have a plan. But you actually have to read to the end to hear it. No, not a plan to switch nuts around. A plan for people to actually have healthcare.

- **Education** (won't kill us but is crucial and can also be part of many public/private partnerships that have worked so well in the past. But K-12 definitely public for all of the community enhancing reasons noted above.)

- **Housing** – The free market has proven that it cannot build enough homes for everyone and has effectively locked out two generations of Americans from the dream of home ownership. And it's not even their fault. The tangle of red tape, regulations, and outlandishly vocal and powerful locals prevent us from building the housing we need. You've heard my solution. Build, build, build, and then when you are done doing that, build, build, build some more. Who better to cut through the red tape than the tapers themselves? Most of this would require public–private partnerships. Fine. Just build until housing is no longer a commodity or a casino. It's a place to live. China has been able to create new cities practically overnight. There is no reason we can't do the same. This is a huge country with incredible natural resources. We have more than enough space to build without harming the environment. And the federal government already owns more than a quarter of the land. The feds own an eye-popping eighty percent of Nevada, sixty-three percent of Utah, and even forty-five percent of California. There is more than enough room. Like everything else, we the people just have to **choose** to do it.

- **Energy** – Ah, the mother of all corrupt clusterfucks. It's more than a century of world-class douchery. We will get into this a bit later. But for the purposes of this section, let's just deal with electric utilities. There is no doubt that a single, publicly owned entity controlling our only source of electric power is an ongoing disaster. They easily overwhelm any local and state attempts at regulation, and they run wild and free, charging whatever the fuck they want and answering to no one. I know it's getting tiresome, but please see *regulatory capture*. **We the people** need to own our electric utility. It's common fucken sense. Or at the very least, form a system that allows for and encourages good old free market competition. The problem with that is that it causes some wasteful duplication of effort and resources that you wouldn't have with a single, publicly owned and operated utility. But it might be worth a shot.

- **Internet** – Yes, I know you don't eat it, and when push comes to shove you don't completely and utterly **NEED** it, but let's dip a toe into the cool refreshing waters of realism and acknowledge that we can't participate in modern life without it. Warning! Boring life anecdote and shameless plug forthcoming: I wrote my first novel, the brilliant and quite attractive *Frum God: The Mostly True Adventures of a Modern Day Messiah* around 2018ish. It is fiction involving the true existence of "cargo cults," real religions that developed on remote South Pacific Islands during World War II. If you add it all up, the research I did to include as many real events as possible took me about five to ten hours. If I had been trying to write that book twenty years ago, I would still be in a library somewhere, getting shushed and dodging homeless people. Or, more likely, I would've just made up a bunch of shit that sounded good. But the point is that I didn't have to. All of the information I needed was literally at my fingertips. Instead of days in the library, it was minutes on my keyboard. The point? Internet service is no longer a **want**. It's a **need** and a **must**, and not just for wannabe novelists. The way we are all so completely and easily finger fucked by Comcast and AT&T just serves to prove that it's a need rather than a want. It's a common good needed by all of us only slightly less than water, power, and healthcare and should be treated the same way and owned by **WE THE PEOPLE.**

There are two of the **Big 4/7** missing from this list: food and clothing. Of course, these are absolute necessities. Clothing is and always will be absurdly plentiful. And we don't need public control of food. I would argue that we already interfere too much. When it comes to food, the public interest is cleanliness, safety, and information—not subsidies. The government should require food to be safe and clean at every level and have law and regulation in place to enforce it. And I think the government should require full disclosure of ingredients and nutritional value. Lastly, we share a common interest in availability of the latest science on nutrition and food as it relates to public health. So it should be the responsibility of the government to make it available. That's it. That's plenty. The free market can do the rest just fine. As we saw earlier, it might even be too good at it.

As I began research for this part, I was shocked to find out how many things the left and right genuinely agreed on. Item by item, specific thing by specific thing, the left and right agreed almost across the board. And I researched dozens of polls from across the political spectrum. So let's try to make a list of things that we already agree we want **government (we the people) to do.**

- **National Defense:** We are all pretty pleased to have a military to protect us. How much we should spend on it is another matter. If a **4 For All** United States eventually morphed into a **4 For All** world, we would clearly have considerably less need for military spending. I'm not saying that everything would become sunshine and roses overnight. But an economically secure world would definitely be a much safer world both from the standpoint of crime and military adventurism. But there would still be a need for a ready, competent military. But certainly not on the scale we need today.

- **Infrastructure:** A lot falls under this heading. But we all need roads, bridges, electrical grids, rural internet, and a bunch of other things. This is where we have been failing for decades because our corporate rulers are not **American** in any meaningful sense and force us to give them tax cuts and subsidies in lieu of actually caring for our own country and its people. We have already seen via Eisenhower's interstate highway system how effective government can be in this area. This is a good time to talk about toll roads. The entire concept is bullshit and should be thrown on the trash heap. We spend billions on toll infrastructure. The result is massive expenditures, lost lives, and more traffic all for what amounts to little more than an accounting trick. Of course, we need money for roads, but tolls are far and away the **least efficient** way to get there. Plus, how do you decide what roads and bridges have a toll and which don't? Republicans, on the rare occasion that they string three or more rational words together, complain about government picking "winners and losers." Well, then what the fuck is this? I have an idea, let's make every road leading to Turtle Dick Mitch McConnell's house a toll road. And don't give me the bullshit argument about we are taxing the people who are using the toll road. You could apply the same stupid logic to every road, including the ones next to my driveway and Turtle Dick's. So let's get rid of all tolls and finance our roads through more rational, cheaper, and fairer ways. Easier said than done at the moment. There's also been a terrifying and corrupt trend of states privatizing roads and tolls in the name of "efficiency." It's nonsense. It's yet another way to funnel public money into private hands that then returns to corrupt politicians to stay in office. Yes, I know, it sounds like a broken record. But it is yet another example of the **Triangle Trade of Corruption.**

- **Schools:** Tough one because, as we know, Republicans have been trying to decimate public schools for decades. They are still pissed about that whole desegregation and no-Jesus thing. Talk about holding a grudge. It will also be tricky to wean them off the dollars they get in kickbacks from the new charter "educational" pillars of the **Triangle Trade of Corruption.** Lately, they have been REALLY pissed about children being taught that white people were a tiny bit meany face to black people for a few centuries. It might hurt little white Johnny's feelings if he learned about lynchings, massacres of entire black towns, and that silly old slavery misunderstanding. During my own lifetime, black people couldn't use a white's only water fountain or stay in the same hotel or neighborhood. Oh, and god forbid if little white Johnny found out that cops have this annoying teensy-weensy habit of shooting or choking black people with little or no provocation. Republicans also get a tad peeved if we forget to tell children how great Jesus is and how pissed off he gets if you say "gay." But despite all that, there is a pretty good majority of not-certifiably-insane Americans that believe teaching children language, math, and science is a halfway decent idea. And just for kicks, let's throw in study after study that show public schools have benefits that go way beyond the classroom. They enable us to concentrate our resources on recruiting and training the best teachers. Public schools are also a foundation of community and civic values and emphasize our commonality. Are public schools perfect? Of course not. All the less so when relentlessly attacked by the powerful and self-interested. But if you want to build a sense of community in a world where we are all becoming further and further isolated from each other, robust public education is the best place to start. Oh yeah, and homeschool kids are always weird. And I recently learned that for many if not most homeschooled victims it got really, really weird. This came from a wannabe cult preacher comically named Bill Gothard (get it Got Hard?). He ended up in a whole bunch of trouble for the customary freaky sexual shit that always seems to come up with religious dipshits. But before that, he was raising a Christian army of homeschooled rednecks. Close to a hundred thousand strong—100,075 if you include the inbred Duggar family.

- **Libraries:** Ben Franklin's twelfth best idea is still pretty popular. And he didn't really *invent* libraries, but he was the key figure in the development of the first lending library in the U.S. in 1757, even before we were even technically the United States. Franklin wasn't known as a socialist, especially since he lived a century before the word "socialism" even existed. But it's hard to find an idea more socialist in nature than libraries. Everybody gives what they have and borrows what they need. And everybody likes libraries. Well, they like the idea of libraries better than actually going to one because almost no one ever goes to a library anymore except homeless people. And they only go because it's the only place they can go to apply for a job on a computer. I myself frequently think about going to the library but then a squirrel walks by and I forget all about it. I have all the attention span of an ADHD toddler. But yeah, almost everyone wants and likes libraries.

- **Police, Justice, and Courts:** Look, there is no argument here. EVERYONE is in favor of order, and everyone is against crime. And no, no one has ever seriously wanted to "defund the police." The phrase was used by a handful of activists and then picked up and used as a political bludgeon for political gain to paint them as irrational and *soft on crime*. The issue is not to defund to police. The issue is to fund some things and change other things to make the job of a policeman doable. Some of you are going to plotz when they find that a big part of the problem traces back to a familiar douchebag: Ronald Reagan. He emptied all the mental hospitals and literally dumped the crazy people onto the streets. Then, he drastically cut funds for social services, including and especially mental health services. He simultaneously flooded neighborhoods with crack while cranking up the punishments for selling and using drugs. All of this was just the start. Republicans and plenty of hapless democrats since Ronnie have picked up the toxic ball and ran with it. Well, more like fatly wobbled with it. The point is that they kept on cutting funds and crucial services for decades. And lest you think I only blame Republicans, the Washington Generals (Democrats) did some very useful kvetching about the whole thing. Bill Clinton stopped by for a while. He was a Democrat ideologically well to the right of Eisenhower and quite possibly Nixon. He was so charming, and so easily blowable that we forgot to notice that he was doing mostly Ronnie Reagan's work. There are some who would say that Clinton was the finest Republican president in history. But he was a link in the unbroken chain of decay that started with Reagan and continues up to today. There was a slight break during the Obama administration but definitely no U-turn. Even Obama would have made an ideologically suitable Republican in the pre-Reagan era. Well, other than the whole not-being-completely-white problem. But the point of this whole thing is that destroying public services has made the job of the modern metro area police officer impossible. They are tasked with enforcing absurd drug laws with even more absurd penalties. They are faced with legions of crazy homeless people roaming the streets in need of help. But instead, the poor cops must arrest them or move them or, as they often do, feed them. They must serve eviction notices to people preyed upon by ruthless, often corporate landlords. They must serve as arbitrators in domestic disputes that wouldn't even have occurred in a country with functioning public services. The point? Their job has become impossible because they are thrust into situations that should not be a part of the role of a policeman but falls to them by default by a hollowed-out infrastructure of social services. And then that turns a bunch of them into lousy cops, and I can hardly blame them. They develop a blue-against-the-world mentality and again, I can hardly blame them. If we want good police, we should go back to letting them do what they were meant to do —police. Instead, they have morphed into a terrified and terrifying militarized force that is a danger to themselves and the community. Oh yeah, remember the community? Can you blame people for being suspicious and fearful of the police? Forget for a moment about being shot or strangled. Just try to imagine what one traffic ticket can do to a poor working citizen. Fines and late penalties have risen drastically more than inflation because revenue-starved cities keep raising them. So a guy pushing a broom for $400 a week gets a couple of tickets. To you and me, it might be inconvenient. For him it might be a death sentence. If he can't afford to pay, he will accrue late fees and penalties, maybe even a bench warrant. Oh, by the way, many cities have privatized fine collections and red-light cameras. So the amount grows larger, and the legal jeopardy intensifies, and the private companies profit, of course kicking back some money to the politicians to keep up the **Triangle Trade of Corruption** again. Can you see the *perverse incentives* at play yet again? The private owners have every incentive to issue as many red-light camera tickets as they can because they are getting a piece of each one. And they are making a massive return on adding late fees and penalties on to the poor bastard. Oh yeah, remember the citizen? The one whose life is being systematically destroyed for profit? Remember him? Maybe he will now end up in a private prison and be even more profitable and do some slave labor as is permitted in the Thirteenth Amendment. So it's a happy and profitable ending after all. The end. Well for him anyway. But can you blame people for being terrified of police? Can you blame police for being terrified of the public? No to both. And yes to blood profit. And blood corruption. This is an absurdly long and sad paragraph. I apologize and I hope you made it through. It was pretty crucial.

Jesus! I have just once again scared and disgusted the shit out of myself and I'm not even sure where to go next. I guess this would be a bad time to bring up that cops now have so much military-grade equipment that they could easily be considered another branch of the military, and our citizens are subject to an ongoing, barely acknowledged form of martial law. No, let's find something light. Yes, ice cream is cold and yummy. Hershey Park has a bunch of cool roller coasters. And we're going to fix this shit. All of it. We can. We Will. Here is one last one.

- **Healthcare:** Fuck it! I'm putting this on the list of things that we agree on because we really actually do. Americans want single-payer healthcare or so-called "Medicare for all." Politicians love to pretend that there is a debate. Well, that debate only involves the politicians and their owners. We the people do want it. We do agree on it. And the only reason we don't get it is because the people who profit from our misery also own our government officials and simply will not allow us to pull the plug on their scam. But I know we agree on it. Why? Because I looked at literally hundreds of polls. The question was posed in slightly different ways in different polls at different times. But more than half of people were in favor of single-payer healthcare in every single poll taken since 2000 except exactly **one**. I checked and rechecked and that is what I found. Could I be wrong? Sure. But even if I am wrong, it wouldn't be by much. The truth is we want it. We just can't have it. YET!

OK. That's enough for now. There are actually a lot more things that we agree on but now, at absolutely no extra charge, completely free . . . the next chapter.

25

BONUS ANALOGIES

You've all read the delightful analogy of capitalism as the most useful and efficient beast of burden when it's properly regulated and fairly free of corruption. But if you act now, you get not one, but two, just as delightful analogies about capitalism and free markets.

First, the board game itself: **MONOPOLY.** The game Monopoly differs from real life in one pretty important way. The game actually has a functioning and uniform set of rules that govern each player. In real life, the rules are made up as they go along by the corporations that own our public officials. But the result of playing the game is similar to what is playing out in real life. One person ends up with everything and everyone else is bankrupt. Yes, of course that's a touch melodramatic and an outright exaggeration, but I wouldn't be exaggerating or lying to say that the world is strongly trending that way. The rich are becoming fewer but much, much richer while the rest of everyone gets noticeably poorer day after day, year after year. The game Monopoly is pretty fun. The real world of monopolies is explicitly dreadful.

But wait, there's more! Call now and receive one last boring analogy about the disaster that is unregulated, free-range capitalism:

Imagine a herd of animals. I don't care, pick one. OK, deer. Imagine some cute little deer. But there's a huge and growing herd of them and no natural predators left to control their growth. Eventually they will eat every leaf off every tree and leave the forest a completely barren wasteland. Fuck! But they're so cute! I saw *Bambi*. But once they have eaten every leaf off every tree, they will soon start eating each other and eventually all will starve and die. I have to admit that was somewhat less cute. So is unregulated capitalism.

I promise we only have one last awful subject left before we begin working on fixing things. But fair warning, it might be the worst of them. Never mind. Healthcare, drugs, and Ford were probably worse . . . maybe.

26

ENERGY

(HEY, WHERE DID MY FENCE GO?)

A while back we talked a bit about the economic concept of *externalities*. I think we discussed that measuring how a free market democracy deals with externalities is a pretty good measure of its political and social health. The idea that private transactions often can and do impose costs on uninvolved parties, and the uninvolved party, more often than not, is the taxpayer—us. Externalities are often, but not always, counted in economic terms and dollar amounts. There are other less tangible and harder to define and measure forms of externalities. Let's take motorcycle helmets as an example. Many states impose helmet mandates on motorcycle riders. They are always controversial and almost always opposed by the riders themselves. I get it. There are some dilemmas here that pit personal freedom against public and personal safety. I'm not a big motorcycle guy, but I understand the whole *wind in my hair, not a care in the world* thing. I understand their passion and their argument. I also understand that the tiniest spot of oil on the pavement can send even the most cautious and safety-conscious rider sliding to the hospital or morgue.

There is no debate about the effectiveness of helmets to

reduce harm. The externalities of a rider who chooses not to wear a helmet are many. This actually turned out to be a pretty good example to use. I apologize in advance, but it's an important point, so I'm going to give you a pretty full plate of the consequences and externalities of helmetless motorcycle riding:

- **Increased healthcare costs:** Motorcyclists who ride without helmets are more likely to suffer severe head injuries in accidents. This leads to higher medical expenses for everyone, which can impact the healthcare system and impose costs on taxpayers.
- **Higher insurance premiums:** With a greater risk of head injuries, riders who don't wear helmets face higher insurance premiums. Insurance companies consider increased risk associated with riding without a helmet when calculating premiums, it also affects those individuals who do wear helmets. So the people who do wear helmets end up paying more because of the people who don't.
- **Emergency services:** Riders without a helmet are more susceptible to serious head trauma in accidents. Dealing with severe injuries requires more extensive emergency response and medical resources, which can strain emergency services and increase response times for other emergencies.
- **Impact on family and dependents:** In the case of a fatal accident, the loss of a motorcycle rider's life can have profound emotional and financial consequences on their family and dependents. Not wearing a helmet increases the likelihood of severe head injuries or death, magnifying the potential negative impact on loved ones. Even non-fatal

injuries can impose financial and emotional burdens that have effects on loved ones and the community.

- **Psychological impact on witnesses:** Witnessing or being involved in a motorcycle accident where the rider was not wearing a helmet can have a lasting psychological impact on bystanders and witnesses. Seeing severe injuries or fatalities can lead to emotional distress and trauma. It can also perpetuate the negative social stigma of cyclists as reckless and careless. Which I guess is kind of deserved.

The reason I tortured you through that whole list is to show that not every consequence or externality can be measured in money. I was also hoping to demonstrate that we as a community are much more connected to each other than we realize. Or care to admit.

I believe in personal liberty and freedom. But many of us seem to have forgotten that with freedom comes responsibility. A free society requires not less, but **more,** of our own personal responsibility. More of a knowledge and understanding of how our actions affect other individuals and our community as a whole. We talked earlier about how people are free to drink alcohol but also how our society has the right to "tax in" the common cost of that behavior. As I said earlier, you can argue that how a democracy manages externalities is a pretty good way to tell how well it functions. Or, as in this instance, fails to function.

A good bit earlier we compared a few common externalities and I quite brazenly promised to deliver unto you the mother of all externalities. Well, here it is in all of its ugly glory.

For this declaration, I'm not going to cite a single source. I'm not going to google shit. I'm not going to the library. I am not going to use any form of AI, and I'm not even going to ask a single person I know or don't know. For this statement I need nothing except this dust-covered keyboard that sits in front of me:

THE QUEST FOR ENERGY HAS CAUSED MORE HARM TO THIS PLANET AND THE PEOPLE ON IT THAN ANYTHING ELSE. THE ONLY OTHER CONTENDER IS FROM THE DEATH AND PSYCHOLOGICAL DISMEMBERMENT CAUSED BY RELIGION. THE DIFFERENCE IS, WE ACTUALLY NEED ENERGY.

This is a vast issue involving war, death, and human and environmental devastation on the widest scale imaginable. The words "oil" and "corruption" are practically interchangeable. And I hardly know where to start. I'm not going to go crazy with this or attempt to give you a complete history, but I will try to hit some of the high–low points. To start with, let's go with a number followed by some context.

$715 billion.

That is the 2022 budget for the U.S. Navy. What does it mean?

A very large portion of that can be considered an *externality* of oil because the U.S. Navy is largely needed to protect shipping lanes for oil, not to mention plastic crap from China for Wal-Mart and Amazon, which oddly enough also involves oil. The Navy is also occasionally called on (along with other branches of the military) to pacify brown people who happen to live where the oil is. Which, it should be noted, kind of pisses those people off and makes them not like or trust us very much. It's kind of understandable. Would you be fond of folks who were raining missiles down on your suburb?

So exactly how much of that can be counted as an externality of oil? Good question. Before we ponder that, let's remember that none of those dollars come from the companies that profit from the oil or the people who buy the oil. The series of transactions that bring the oil from the ground into your gas tanks pay exactly zero dollars of whatever that amount is.

It is the taxpayer who pays for the Navy. Yes, some of those taxpayers are also part of the final transaction involving the oil, which could be filling their gas tanks, paying their electric bills, or buying petroleum-based lube to have anal sex with an alarmingly lifelike Rupert Murdoch inflatable doll. But even then, they are paying nowhere close to the true cost of the oil they are consuming. The taxpayer is picking up the tab for the Navy. Most experts agree on a solid half, $367 billion, of the Navy budget to be costs of protecting oil. But that's just a start. When you factor in other branches of the service, you end up with somewhere around a trillion-dollar tax bill dumped annually on the taxpayer. Not that I begrudge the military or the brave people who serve in it. In fact, it could be regarded as an extremely successful example of socialism. They are clothed, fed, and housed socially. They receive free healthcare for life. I'm not begrudging them that, just pointing out that the whole shebang is pretty fucken socialist. And nobody seems to mind. I certainly don't. I admire anybody who chooses that life. It's easy to talk a good patriotic game. It's a whole other thing to put your life on the line.

The whole military could be considered a form of Hillbilly Welfare. Now that I think about it I don't even need to bother with this book. Just conscript everybody. Send every American a "pick a branch" letter. In my case, it would be "Welcome to the Army" because my whole family served in the Army. I know I'm way off subject now, but I am the first male in my family in at least four generations to not serve. Oddly enough, that does make me a little sad. I would gladly have served, if asked. But when I was eighteen, I had a very busy schedule of smoking weed and learning to throw a jai lai ball, often at the same time. Last thing before we get back to work, I said four generations and that is true, but my great-grandfather was in the Russian cavalry so you can decide if that counts or not. Sorry, got off topic there for a bit again. Back to work.

The environmental externalities of oil and coal run into many trillions of dollars all on their own. The people who profit from oil and those that consume it cover exactly zero dollars of the costs of this damage.

Just the two things above already make energy the mother of all externalities, and we're still just scratching the surface. We haven't even started drilling yet. Sorry, couldn't help it. Just too easy. Let's leave money for a moment and talk . . .

Global political stability, or more often, instability. The quest for energy is always the number one driver (sorry, can't help it) of geopolitical instability and war. It's a massive subject and one that we can start with a silly question.

Earlier on, we brought Genghis Khan back from the dead to have a look at the slot machine created in his honor. Now we're going to dig up any expert car mechanic who died a century ago. Here's the question:

Could our zombie mechanic fix the engine in a modern gas-fueled car? In other words, could he find his way around the modern internal combustion engine?

The answer, in large part, is yes. Sure, he'd have to work his way around the computers. It would take him about a half hour to figure out fuel injectors. The AC unit would be completely foreign to him. But yes, assuming none of his zombie parts fell off, yes, he could fix it. He would be able to perform some useful work on the basic components of the internal combustion engine that has changed very little during his century in the afterlife.

Yes, I know that we are slowly evolving to electric vehicles, but that doesn't change the point. The fact is that the basic technology of the automobile was fundamentally unchanged for more than a century. Can you think of any other technology that remained frozen in time like that? There might actually be a couple of things. The wheel, for instance.

But the world of energy is where you will have no problem finding real, actual conspiracies. Oil has controlled the world and those who profit from it have been ruthless and successful at keeping it that way for a long, long time.

I can't even come close to covering all the gory details of oil's bloody rein over the planet. So let's settle for some low lights:

- Oil companies, rubber tire manufacturers, and car makers conspired to kneecap public transportation in the United States for decades. They wanted to sell lots of cars and gas and rubber tires. They bought up and dismantled public trolley systems in city after city and sold off the easements to make sure they could never be reassembled. In doing so, they practically created the modern American suburb. Which is another entire shit show. It would be nearly impossible to grasp the external costs to taxpayers for just this one single phenomenon, but it's vast. *Who Framed Roger Rabbit?*
- Stanley Whittingham, a scientist working for Exxon, created the first lithium-ion battery in the 1970s. At first, Exxon embraced the new technology but quickly changed gears, fired Whittingham, and refused other scientists access to the new technology. The technology had to start over from scratch. By the way, Whittingham actually won a Nobel Prize for it. That single decision by Exxon pushed the development of electric cars back by two decades or more. And to be honest, it still puzzles me. If Exxon had chosen to *own it* instead of *kill it,* they may very well have made **even more money**

than they had in the oil business. They would have had a huge head start and made billions before anyone had a chance to catch up. And just try to imagine how much better off the world would be politically, economically, and environmentally. I guess in hindsight, the *sure thing* of oil won out in the Exxon boardroom. And the world lost out. Big time.

- There are dozens of instances of oil companies buying up and burying patents for technology that could replace either oil or the internal combustion engine.

There is so much more, most of which you probably already know and don't even want to think about it. And I can't blame you. War, corruption, and geopolitical instability. What makes me crazy about the whole thing is that so much of it was so easily avoidable.

This morning as I write this, the Saudis completed their takeover of professional golf. The Saudi owned LIV Golf merged with the PGA. In the moment, it is shocking news, but the writing has been on the wall for a while now. A little over a year ago, the then new LIV Golf started throwing absurd amounts of money at top pros, trying to lure them away in hopes of competing with the PGA. Now they own the whole thing. For some reason, all of this reminds me of *The Godfather's* Michael Corleone trying to convince his wife Kay that in five years the Corleone family will be completely legitimate.

Something similar has been going on with European football leagues. That's soccer to people like you and me. Deep-pocketed shady oil oligarchs have been buying up the cash-strapped teams. I don't know a ton about soccer, but I have friends that live it, as many Europeans do. And it is their opinion that the game has lost its soul. Now golf has too.

The first time anybody in the U.S. noticed that oil is a pain in the ass was in 1973 when Israel kicked the shit out of a bunch of Arab countries in the Yom Kippur War. It's also the first time regular people ever heard of OPEC, which is basically the Arab oil exporters. The Arabs didn't much care for the U.S. supporting Israel and stopped selling us oil for a while. The famous oil embargo.

There were gas lines and panic and suddenly an average American might be able to find some of these countries on a map. Which is my way of telling this truth. The U.S. wouldn't give a flying fuck about any of those countries if we didn't need the oil. There are almost two hundred sovereign nations on the planet, and I'd be willing to bet the average American couldn't name a third of them, at most. But we've all heard of Iran and Iraq, etc., for one reason and one reason alone: oil.

So back to what makes me crazy about it. In the decade following the first oil shock, average miles per gallon in the United States doubled and then flattened out almost completely until just a few years ago. It even slightly declined between 1985 and 2005. Recently, the hybrids and then fully electric vehicles started skewing the average higher. In general numbers, average miles per gallon went from about twelve in 1975 to about twenty-four in 1985 and then pretty much just stayed there.

It's important to remember that by 1985 it was fully understood by almost everybody what a clusterfuck the Middle East is, was, and might always be. We knew damn well we were vulnerable. We knew damn well oil was finite. We knew damn well that giving money to Arab states, especially Saudi Arabia, was the exact same thing as handing it to terrorists. We didn't know exactly who was doing what with who, but we knew in general that depending on Arab oil was bad and making shitty regimes rich was even worse.

The technology existed as early as the 1970s to make gas

cars that would get thirty, forty, maybe even fifty miles per gallon if we wanted to. And if we had done that, the average American would know just as much about Syria and Lebanon as we do about Comoros, Bhutan, and my personal favorite, Djibouti. Which is to say, we never would have heard of Syria or Lebanon or Iran or Iraq. And yes, Djibouti is a real country. So are the other two that I already forgot.

Yes, cars with that kind of mileage would have been sluggish and would maybe only have had a top speed of eighty miles per hour or so, but so fucken what? The shittiest thing about them would have been that it would take them fifteen to twenty seconds to reach top legal speeds. That's a bit of a pain in the ass, especially compared with what we are used to, but they would still have gotten us boringly from home to work and back in the same amount of time. Slow boring cars would still have functioned every bit as effectively to provide actual reliable transportation. If we had chosen to drive cars that got forty miles per gallon or more, we would have had virtually **NO NEED** to import any oil from anybody, ever. Oil would have been just another boring commodity and not the explosive geopolitical and terrorist-funding force it became. Yes, cars would have been boring, but in exchange, we would have gotten a much more boring world. And when it comes to the world, boring is good. Ask anybody who was in the World Trade Center on 9/11 if they would have preferred a little boredom.

Instead, the focus went from fuel efficiency to more horsepower and from cars to SUVs and trucks. Don't get me wrong, I like trucks. I like trucks, but I like peace better. And I know we still would've needed some trucks, of course. But I'm not joking. Had we chosen to, we could have made Saudi Arabia every bit as irrelevant to the average American as Djibouti, which I still think is a great name for a nightclub emcee, opening for Pitbull.

The reasons why we didn't choose that option are as dense and complex as why we haven't yet built a **4 For All** world. Plenty of corruption. Plenty of greed. A pretty good dash of treason. A fair amount of the fragile male ego, and the marketing that stokes and strokes it. Cars have never truly been about transportation. Almost from the moment they were invented, they became part of who we are, who we want to be, and what we want people to think we are. On the extreme male side was the Corvette or Porche, always the antidote for the typical mid-life crisis. It's the equivalent of a woman choosing that $2,000 Coach purse when the $10 Amazon bag will perform the exact same function.

We didn't choose oil freedom and peace because we didn't **want** to. We prefer the value of the soothing emotional gifts of a fast car to the more ephemeral and seemingly unconnected concept of relative world peace and disarming the bad guys.

But it was, in fact, a huge deal. It is impossible to overestimate. Giving trillions of dollars to shitty leaders of captive countries caused harm, bloodshed, corruption at the highest levels, and the genuine **need** to spend ourselves silly with the military. The monetary externalities can be measured in tens of trillions. The measure in blood is priceless.

But one of the hardest externalities to measure is also the most important one, **women**. We funded those Wahabi twats that had, and still have, a Stone Age view of women. The suffering of women under these shitty regimes that we propped up and still prop up with our petro-dollars cannot be overestimated.

When economists and sociologists look around the world, they find one commonality, almost without exception. You can know how well a country functions politically and economically simply by how the women fare in that society. The more women are free and have control of their own lives, the better off the country is. Again, almost without exception. The overall welfare of a state can almost always be determined by a single indicator: reproductive rights. Most places where women have a choice thrive. Where they don't, society doesn't succeed. The loss of abortion rights in the U.S. is a nice wide line for our drive into third-world status, a status we now richly deserve for allowing the white Christian nationalists the keys to our kingdom.

It is the Saudis that created, funded, and deployed untold millions of religious fanatics. Using our own money to do it, Saudi Arabia attacked us on 9/11. As you will see later, they corrupted our government and leaders. They have played both ends against the middle for more than a century. And now they are trying to buy up the things we love in an effort to put a happy face on their ugly evil. Rarely do I speak in simple declarations, but this is one of those times. Saudi Arabia is the bad guy. They are not the only bad guys. But they are THE bad guys.

But there's plenty of blame to spread around.

If we had found the political will to bite the bullet and force the production of boring cars that got at least forty miles per gallon cars, American car makers would have faced a period of uncertainty as they adapted to those mileage standards that **should** have been imposed on the grounds of national security. With the benefit of hindsight, I can say it would have been more than worth it for the taxpayer to subsidize the automakers during my fantasy transition of the seventies and eighties. And they do make a fuck load of money selling trucks. But a public investment in the domestic auto industry in exchange for very high mileage standards would have brought very good returns for the taxpayer and the domestic auto industry in the long run. It's impossible to estimate the benefits we would have received from that investment, but it would have been massive. Wars would have been avoided. The climate and environment would be in much better shape. We may very well have never learned the word terrorism. And, I can't prove it, but I'd be willing to bet that the events of 9/11 would never have occurred. If for no other reason than they wouldn't have had American petro-dollars to fund it, nor many of the reasons to have even wanted to do it.

On 9/11, we were attacked by Saudi Arabia. There are people who might argue that statement and they would be wrong. It is indisputable that fifteen of the nineteen hijackers were Saudi nationals. What is not widely understood is that Al-Qaeda itself was a creation of the Saudi government and educational system. The Saudi's funded schools that taught an extreme and violent sect of Islam known as Wahhabism. Osama bin Laden claimed responsibility for the attack through the terrorist group Al-Qaeda. Bin Laden himself was a Saudi, born to a very prominent Saudi family. Here's where the allegedly treasonous part comes in. The Bin Laden family and Bush family had been friendly associates for more than a century. That in itself is shady, but not necessarily treasonous.

George W. Bush is a nice man with (and I'm being generous here) an average IQ. As a young man, he had a bit of a substance abuse problem. Like many young men born to prominent families, he had plenty of rope with which to hang himself. Tangent alert: When I was growing up and to this day, the very expensive, very fancy high school for rich kids in my area was known as the place that had the most and best drugs. I doubt that they were an outlier. I would expect that this is common across the spectrum of expensive private and boarding schools.

So little George was a bit of a hellion but not too bad, certainly not by modern standards. He had only two arrests on his record by the time his dad kept him out of Vietnam and greased him safely into the Texas Air National Guard. According to his military record, sometimes young George actually showed up for duty. Other times, not so much.

When it comes to trying to do clean research on this stuff, it's incredibly difficult and murky. The zone of symbiosis between the Bush and Bin Laden families is most definitely flooded with shit. But there is no argument that the two families have business and political ties that reach beyond a century. So there are some things we know for sure, without dispute.

- According to *The Denver Post* and other sources, in 1978, W Bush and Osama bin Laden's brother, Salem bin Laden, founded Arbusto Energy, an oil company based in Texas. The name was extraordinarily accurate as Arbusto went busto, running up millions in debt that far outweighed its assets. There were murky mergers, sales, and transfers through various companies such as Harken and Spectrum 7 Energy. Eventually all were bailed out by the Carlyle Group, a company that had both Bin Ladens and Bushes on its board. Young George walked away from his less-than-worthless company with a few million dollars with which to start his new career in politics.
- Carlyle's 2001 investor conference took place on **September 11, 2001.** In the weeks following the meeting, it was reported that Shafiq bin Laden, a member of the Bin Laden family, had been the guest of honor, and majority investor in Carlyle managed funds.
- On September 11, 2001, members of the Carlyle Group, including Bush Sr. and his former Secretary of State James Baker, were meeting at the Ritz Carlton Hotel in Washington, D.C., again with Shafiq bin Laden.
- While all flights were halted following the terrorist attacks of 9/11, there was one exception made: The

White House authorized planes to pick up 140 Saudi nationals, including twenty-four members of the Bin Laden family. They brought them back to Saudi Arabia, where they would be safe. They were never interrogated. In other words, the only people in the world who could fly on 9/12, were Bin Ladens.

We could go on this way all day finding corruption and chicanery that led to incredibly bloody and expensive consequences. W, along with Congress, used 9/11 as an excuse to pass the ridiculously titled USA Patriot Act. Why do I call it ridiculous? Because this 342-page piece of legislation was the largest CONTRACTION of civil liberties in American history. By their own admission, less than ten percent of Congress even read the fucken thing before passage. It contained police state provisions that would make a dictator blush.

George W. Bush said famously "they hate us for our freedom," just as he and Congress took many of our freedoms away permanently. The police and surveillance state created that day continues to this day.

And no discussion of this repulsive subject would be complete without this guy: Richard Colvin Reid. You might remember this genius. The odds are very good that he has affected your life. This particular jerkoff is the reason you have to take your shoes off at the airport. In December 2001, with the scab of 9/11 not yet healed, he tried to set his shoe on fire on board a flight from Paris to Miami (of course, because if something silly and dangerous happens, there is always a Florida connection). The shoe contained a small amount of explosive that Einstein was trying to detonate, but it was wet and almost impossible to ignite. He was easily subdued by passengers and crew. He was trussed up and sedated by the time the plane diverted to Boston Logan International Airport for moron disposal.

So for more than twenty years, all of us have been taking our shoes off at airports because of this one asshole. And flying, which was already a nightmare, had somehow found a way to suck even worse. The entire performance of **security theater** at airports would be funny if it wasn't so awful. Any expert on the subject will gladly explain to you that all the hassle you go through at the airport makes you only the tiniest bit safer, if at all. Almost all of it truly is a performance, a demonstration meant to show how hard we are trying. But the truth is that reasonably competent people with bad intentions can still do terrible things very easily. Consider that even Reid, quite possibly the least competent bad guy imaginable, still succeeded at making life just a bit worse for every person who has flown in the last two decades.

Tangent alert: Two of the 9/11 hijackers worked at the Circle K store down the street from my house that I visited every single day to feed my Diet Coke addiction. I recognized at least a half dozen of them that lived in my neighborhood.

This seems like a good time to remind you that if cars were legally required to get forty miles per gallon by 1985, none of this shit would've happened. None of it. All of this, every last bit of it, is an *externality* of oil.

So how would the young dimwit W respond to the terror attacks of 9/11? You know, the attacks that were orchestrated by a man whose family has been friends with your family for generations? The family that bailed you out when you somehow managed to be the only person to LOSE MONEY in the oil business. Well, of course everybody knows that when you are attacked by a country, you go and kill that country's enemies. Of course, I am joking. That would be idiotic. But that is exactly what we did. Saudi Arabia attacked us, so we attacked Iraq and Afghanistan, sworn blood enemies of the Saudi royal family. It is impossible to overestimate how ridiculous this was. And this is NOT a case of hindsight.

In the moment, our military and intelligence community knew it was ridiculous and said so, over and over. As far as Afghanistan goes, the military knew there were no real military targets in Afghanistan. One member of the Joint Chiefs of Staff put it this way, *All we can do in Afghanistan is turn big pieces of rubble into smaller pieces of rubble.* That's not to say that we shouldn't have gone after Bin Laden himself in Afghanistan, but the military would have chosen to do so through a combination of diplomacy, tactical strikes, and drones. But W repeatedly prevented, understaffed, and undermined efforts to get Bin Laden.

Which is actually pretty funny when you think about it. Bush claimed he couldn't find Bin Laden, a six-foot-six-inch Arab schlepping around a kidney dialysis machine. Sounds silly when you put it that way, doesn't it? But it was every bit that silly and then some. Because it was almost comically easy for Obama to find and kill Bin Laden, but it was years later. Almost makes you think that the tiny little, fetal alcohol syndrome baby W wasn't really trying. And my apologies to victims of fetal alcohol syndrome. It sucks. And George's mother Barbara was a nice lady. She just didn't know any better at the time that she was drinking poor George into a lifetime of stupidity.

Now let's talk Iraq and Saddam Hussein. He was a douche and I shed not a single tear for his demise. But he had nothing to do with 9/11 or any other terrorist attack anyone can think of. Nor did anyone even remotely believe that he had weapons of mass destruction. It was a joke. And everybody in intelligence and military circles knew it **at the time**. Bin Laden himself hated Saddam Hussein and rarely missed an opportunity to say so.

You know what, I'm just tired of this crap. We got attacked. We got pissed off. We took it out by hurting our own citizens and made ourselves forever much less free. We attacked THE

ENEMIES of the country that attacked us and made them even richer and more powerful to the point where they can buy up the things we love, like soccer, golf, and a big chunk of U.S. real estate.

If anyone not named Bush was president on 9/11, we would have destroyed Saudi Arabia and toppled it's disgusting, murderous royal family in about twenty minutes. The world would have been an incredibly better place. The only reason we didn't was that the *Bin Ladens* and Saudi royals own Bush and his family. If you aren't getting the picture yet, it's on you. Good luck. Make sure to take your fucken shoes off at the airport.

This has already been a long section. And if I was going to fully explore it, it could go on a lot longer. Coal has its own very long and horrible history of death, disease, and labor abuse. And holy shit, if I were to even try to estimate the externalities of coal. The costs to the taxpayer for the use of coal have been truly breathtaking. Heh? Did you see what I did there? Breathtaking, get it? Air pollution and shit. Well, no one ever died from smog. Except, yeah, they have. A lot.

We're going to use the old micro/macro approach to get out of this quickly. Actually, there is no *old micro/macro approach*, I just made it up. But here it is. People really do die from air pollution. Here's the micro, meaning a single incident.

The Great Smog of London in 1952. From December 5 to 9, a thick layer of smog enveloped the city. Depending on whose numbers you use, somewhere between four thousand and ten thousand people died during those four days. Medium- and longer-term deaths were harder to track but were at least an additional ten thousand. Burning coal was the main culprit. But the combination of unusual cold and peculiar atmospheric conditions trapped the fumes close to the ground. Funny thing though. The people who sold the coal that killed all those people didn't pay a dime—pardon me—a shilling. I probably don't have to keep reminding you at this point, but every one of those deaths counts as an *externality* of coal.

People died. And I don't feel good about this. But we also need to consider the monetary costs incurred and paid by the British people from this event. Remember, the seller of the coal *earned* money and paid for no part of the result. Let's try to imagine in pounds and shillings what it cost the British taxpayers at that time. It had to be massive. I'd be willing to bet there are still costs from that event still being paid by the British people to this day. There were babies and toddlers from those days that are still alive today and whose lungs **still** bear the scars of those four days in 1952. Treating those remaining victims of an event seventy years ago isn't cheap.

That was the micro. Granted it was a pretty big micro, but it was still just micro. You're not going to like the macro. According to the World Health Organization, outdoor air pollution is estimated to cause around 4.2 million premature deaths worldwide each year. This includes deaths from various respiratory and cardiovascular diseases, as well as lung cancer.

And even that is still nowhere close to the big momma macro: climate change. Almost all of the current and future events related to climate change and/or global warming have their roots in energy consumption. Look, I'm not judging anyone. I'm not sitting here telling you to turn off your AC or trade in your F-150 for a scooter, or worse, a Tesla. My air conditioning is on and I'm casting no stones. But what is is. And the truth is that the story of climate change is the story of energy.

Now, spend the rest of your natural days at Hotel Earth trying to figure out what global warming is going to cost you and what it is already costing you. Happy news for investors though, taxpayers don't reclaim a penny of the costs inflicted on them from any of the externalities of energy. The mostly foreign companies keep raking in the dough and we keep picking up the tab for:

- **Rising temperatures:** Average global temperatures have been increasing, leading to heatwaves and more frequent and intense heat events that are killing actual people. More every year. And not just in places that Trump calls shit holes. More than twenty thousand people died from extreme heat during the summer of 2022 in Western Europe, a place not yet commonly thought of as a shit hole.
- **Melting ice and rising sea levels:** I'm going with the *glass half full* approach with this one. Lots of very nice people in Pennsylvania and Nevada will eventually have ocean-view properties.
- **Extreme weather events:** We can look forward to more frequent and severe extreme weather events, including hurricanes, droughts, wildfires, and heavy rainfall. As a *Florida man,* I have lived through some 749 hurricanes. I made that up. Realistically it's more like thirty-five or so, including the really fun one when I watched a six-foot section of what had been my fence go flying into the heavens *Wizard of Oz* style. This a few seconds after watching five palm trees topple into each other like dominos and land in my pool. The pool was less than impressed and proceeded to pop out of the ground like a zit. Who says climate change can't be fun?
- **A bunch of other shit:** Really, a lot more. And this chapter is already way too long, so let's just say there's a lot more and some we don't even know are coming. I'll just leave you with acid rain because it's particularly creepy and was never the working title of the *Prince* movie.

What makes it even more fun is that the foreign investors we make rich are now using our money to buy up our real estate, which is still seen as a safe haven for foreign capital. It's really swell for the investors but ever so slightly less so for Americans. Because now we get to rent back from them the houses and apartments that used to be ours.

And it's interesting how a discussion of energy ends with real estate. How Americans are being not so slowly squeezed into becoming serfs in their own country.

I spent a few hours last night sorting through a mountain of statistics on property values and rents and, even more importantly, housing costs as a *percentage of income.*

It's ugly. Very, very ugly. There is not a single metro area in the United States where a person making the region's *average* wage can afford a two-bedroom apartment. Mind you, I said *average* wage, not *minimum* wage. We are being priced out of life. Eighty percent of Americans are one lost paycheck or one illness away from homelessness. Now just consider how many are able to even give a thought to their future while they struggle just to survive. And these are the healthy, working people.

I'm going to leave you with the story of one single-family home in a suburb in Chicago. It was considered a mansion when it was built in 1950. It sold for $6,300 back then. In 2023 inflation-adjusted dollars it would be $95,000. It's on the market now. The asking price is $2.2 million. This is not sustainable. We are in big trouble. But now, finally, it is time to fix it. Well, first, we will talk about how it's impossible to fix.

27

IMPOSSIBLE TO FIX

(BUT NOT REALLY)

Together, we have spent all these pages discussing just how bad things have gotten. We have gone item by item and tried to show how they tie together. We have shown that we have created a world that has spun out of control and is in imminent danger of spinning off into impoverished chaos.

Honestly, it's been pretty depressing so far, even for me. I've tried to lighten it up wherever possible with my sparkling wit, but some things just won't fucken sparkle, no matter how I might try to polish them up. A **Big 4/7** world won't be easy to create. There are just too many forces against us. Notice I say *us*, as if to say that I have won you over and we are now on the same team. I hope that is true. But even if it isn't true, you have made it this far. Stay with me just a bit longer. We are going to need a lot of help to climb out of this hole, but first we have to stop digging it deeper.

As we have seen, a corporate oligarchy of our own creation stands astride our nation and our world. Craven, amoral beasts have broken their bonds and run roughshod over our land and lives. They now hold power that is near absolute. That was all just a bit flowery and poetic. But also, sadly, quite true.

Worse, they have used much of that power to divide us against each other for their own gain. And never have they been more successful. We face a group of our own countrymen who have been stripped of all reason. They have been deprived of the oxygen of reality for so long that they now stand asphyxiated, dumbfounded, and unable to take a breath of reality, even when given to them in its purest forms.

These victims are just people. They are, or were, our friends, our neighbors, our families. For forty years they have been fed a steady sensationalized diet of racist white Christian tropes, fear, hatred of immigrants, and a corporate ideology that changes only as dominant corporate power itself changes. But one form of programming has been remarkably consistent: The government itself is either evil, incompetent, or both—and definitely not to be trusted. The federal deficit is always used to prevent any spending on anything that will enable or improve the lives of citizens but becomes irrelevant when it comes to paying subsidies or even further cutting the taxes of corporations and the ultra-rich.

Any spending on the country itself or its citizens is demonized as socialism, while tax cuts and subsidies to corporations are deemed necessary because they *create jobs*, which I would consider wildly hilarious if it weren't so sad. And, as Eisenhower tried to warn us, the beast of defense contractors always demands to be fed. And they are indeed being fed. To the point where U.S. defense spending is forty percent of the total for the entire world. Three times more than China, ten times more than Russia.

Rupret Murdoch and Roger Ailes used Fox News to detach viewers from reality and enclose them in a bubble. It was successful because fear is always more compelling than understanding. Anger is always more compelling than nuance. And what you want to believe is always more soothing than reality.

There is a *war* on Christmas if someone dares to say "happy holidays." Gay people don't want equal rights, they want special treatment and to "groom" your little Johnny and make him gay. That alone should be enough to convince a not-crazy person that Fox people are fucken nuts. Short of rape (you know rape, it's what Catholic priests do to little boys), you can't make someone gay any more than you can make someone straight. And any rational person would never care what any consenting adult does with another consenting adult. *Who gives a shit?* Is my response to any sexual issue that involves consenting people over the age of eighteen. Gay people want to get married? Fine, who gives a shit? Somebody wants to be trans-gender, transexual, or trans-anything? Fine, who gives a shit? Love who you want, and strive for happiness any way you can in this harsh and demanding world. As long as everyone is of age and nobody gets hurt, do whatever you want.

And since we detoured into this subject, I have to get this off my chest. I don't think anyone born with a schlong should compete in female sports. Female athletes are finally starting to get the respect and exposure they always deserved. And now some mediocre schlong bearers are going to screw it all up. Be who you want. Call yourself whatever you want. Love whoever you want. But just like in democracy, there does need to be a couple of rules of common sense. In public restrooms, if you wield a schlong, go to the men's room. In sports, compete in the men's division if you happen to have a schlong. If you were born schlonged but decided to de-schlong along the way. please still consider yourself still schlonged for the purposes of sports and public restrooms. I don't think it's too much to ask. It's kind of just courteous civility.

For those of us outside the Fox bubble, some good things have come along. We are profoundly aware of and sensitive to issues of racism, misogyny, and gay rights. Even some of us outside the bubble may say that, in some ways, we may have become overzealous and overly sensitive to these issues.

I think you can make an argument that we have made it harder to have a conversation for fear of offending someone or being "canceled," though I believe that the threat of being "canceled" is overblown. Nobody is being brought in front of a firing squad for what they say, and the government isn't prosecuting people for saying stupid things, so there is no First Amendment issue here. It's anyone's right to say any stupid thing they want. And it's my right and your right to call it stupid.

But you know what? We're human, so we're going to err in our treatment of sensitive issues sometimes. I would much prefer to err toward too much consciousness rather than too little. For instance, I would rather go too far in teaching about the horror of slavery, the utter failure of reconstruction and the lingering social and economic effects of racism. It is much worse to risk not going far enough. No one wants people alive today to feel shame for the actions of their ancestors. But it would be criminal to neglect and ignore how vast the crimes and how real consequences were. Even to this day.

Those of us outside the bubble have made progress in other ways as well. I see evidence of people trying to find ways to break the links of generational curses like spousal abuse, child abuse, addiction, and racism. As a society, we still have a long way to go, but just the fact that so many of us are aware of it is reason enough for hope. Now try to imagine how far we could all go in a **4 For All** world. Imagine a world where we weren't all wandering around in perpetual survival mode because we know nothing else. No other way to live. But for now, let's get back to our friends locked **in** the Fox bubble and **out** of reality.

OK, so their brainwashing went on for forty years right under our collective noses. Those of us outside of the Fox bubble merely laughed it off or barely noticed. For most of us, reality itself remained unchallenged. Some of us made fun of the victims we would sometimes encounter at family gatherings. It was just some crazy old uncle. But the bubble kept growing bigger and louder. There were new voices that were even angrier. And soon that audience itself would demand nothing less than ever angrier screams.

I hate to say this, but I can't help but think that the election of Barack Obama had something to do with the mainlining and mainstreaming of racism and white Christian supremacist doctrine. Not that I'm blaming Obama—he was a perfectly good *real*, very slightly left of center president and the best we could have hoped for. But for tens of millions of people his election was the equivalent of *shit getting real* for the first time. To many white people, civil rights and equality was great, to a point. There was some sort of weird visceral reaction from people who were not particularly or overtly racist. Or perhaps they themselves weren't even aware of their own lingering subconscious racism. But there, for the first time, before their very eyes was a black man in the Oval Office. And he wasn't holding a servant's tray. There was a black man on Air Force One. And he wasn't loading the luggage. Something about that triggered a kind of racist backlash that made the "birther" fields even greener for Trump to graze. And graze he did. It's hard to quantify, which I have shown in the haplessly flailing way I've tried to describe it. But it was real.

Court documents and reporting have shown that many of those Fox News voices and others were those of performers, essentially actors who created and acted out very profitable personas. It worked, and the victims were told exactly what they wanted to hear and had come to expect. They were even told that they were victim of any number of always changing slates of made-for-TV villains. They were always under attack from forces who were coming to get their guns. Socialists who will turn us into a nightmarish Soviet Union or Venezuela. Or drag queens coming for your little Johnny, who is under attack by homos, critical race theory, and "leftists."

There was a never-ending parade of fear and anger. And to hold the attention of their audiences, the stakes and lies always had to grow bigger and wilder.

Then came Trump and Steve Bannon. Trump was the first to understand this group of victims that had been perfectly groomed for him. He understood that at this point these people could be convinced of absolutely anything.

What I am saying now is largely speculation, but I believe Trump was insolvent when he decided to run for president in 2016. I also believe that was why he so fervently protected his tax returns, despite the fact that it had become standard for any serious candidate to publicly release their tax returns. He didn't want to ruin what was left of his image by letting people see he was broke. But Trump knew it was a new world. He could say or do anything without consequence, and the campaign funds would salve his wounded finances.

Remember, it is known that he'd run out of people to lend him money. He'd burned thousands of creditors. He'd actually found a way to bankrupt casinos. Trust me, I'm in that business. It's not easy to do. U.S. banks wouldn't touch him. Only Russian oligarchs would lend to him in exchange for the "legitimate" and "luxurious" Trump brand. I don't think he expected to win. He was running for his financial life. And he knew that, with his audience, he could say or do anything. He was playing with house money.

Bannon was the final piece of the puzzle. The man who ran the ultra-right white Christian nationalist *Breitbart* knew the way. Yeah, you know. **FLOOD THE ZONE WITH SHIT!** Now it was more than just the Fox News captives. You could get the message, any message, out to the world. Just make up what you want to be true, repeat it over and over again until it's real—or at least real enough to confound the genuine news media—because now, if they want to be considered *news*, they have to report *both sides* of every ginned up and nonsensical issue. Both sides became a competition with reality on one side and whatever dogshit Trump, Bannon, and the right-wing media made up on the other.

They had effectively castrated the real media and turned all reality into subjectivity and self-promotion. It is estimated that the free advertising Trump got for saying ludicrous things was worth more than $1 billion in the run up to the 2016 election.

I know I keep repeating it, but "flood the zone with shit" is probably the single most traitorous, treacherous, and disgusting thing done in the history of the republic. It makes Benedict Arnold seem downright patriotic by comparison. Democracy simply cannot exist when we don't have a common set of facts that we can even base disagreements on, let alone work through them.

Trump brilliantly and ruthlessly recognized and capitalized on the world that had been created by Ailes, Bannon, Murdoch, and the like. And I recognize and salute his cunning and instincts. And Jerry, he is the best of all liars, because he truly believes it himself. All Trump has ever cared about is Trump and getting attention for Trump. He is a truly sick and dangerous man, but he was not the cause of our demise. He was the result. Forty years of evil preceded where we are now, perched on the precipice of doom, our toes curled over its edge.

But now comes the good part.

We can fix it. It's only about thirty percent of the population that is trapped in the bubble. That, of course, is not enough to win elections. The Republicans know that. All but the most delusional Republicans know that their policies, or lack thereof, are unpopular. They have won exactly one popular vote for the presidency since 1988. That was in 2008. Counting every vote, they have not won a majority in Senate voting since 2014. They haven't won a majority of House of Representatives votes since 2010. Just to make it clear, I am talking about adding up all the red and blue votes cast nationwide in those elections for House, Senate, and Presidency.

To put it simply, Republicans know and have known for quite some time that they have drifted way outside the mainstream. They know it's going to become harder and harder to win any election. A rational reaction would be to forsake the craziness of the fascist right wing and move somewhere closer to the middle. In fact, that's how the two-party system had usually functioned for two centuries. If either party drifted too far from the middle, they were punished at the ballot box. They would learn their lesson and move more toward the middle.

So what changed? Why do Republicans repeatedly continue to double down on crazy. I think there are two parts to the answer and they both suck.

First, they created and nurtured this core group, which for sake of simplicity we will just call "The Foxies." Although at this point it's far bigger than just them. They created this group of scared, angry, mostly white, and aging people. But somewhere along the line they lost control of the monster they created. That core group began demanding that they go further and further off the deep end. These poor fuckers had been fed a steady diet of racism, white supremacy, anti-science, anti-government, anti-gay, evangelical white Christian dogma for so long that it took on a life of its own. So much so that they don't even trust themselves. If you so much as think about compromising on anything with anyone, your political life is over. And as we will see in a moment, perhaps your actual life as well. They had so demonized Democrats and *leftists* that they could never compromise or actually govern.

This is really something new in American politics. The Republicans have become terrified of their own base. The very group they helped create. And with very good reason. Remember, it was Mike Pence they wanted to hang on January 6th. Yes, they took a shit on Nancy Pelosi's desk, but they actually wanted to **hang** Mike Pence.

Just consider that last sentence for a moment. Republican insurrectionists wanted to hang the Vice President of the United States of **their own party**! First of all, let's talk Mike Pence. This is a man so aggressively dull that I can't work up enough energy to hate him. But I should. And you should too. But not for the reasons that the fascist mob at the Capitol wanted to hang him. They wanted to hang him because he would not cooperate in Trump's effort to dismantle the Constitution and just give Trump the Presidency. The dumb fuck actually did the right thing for once and refused to destroy our democracy. The fact that someone even had to do that, and that we have to give him credit for that, should scare the shit out of you. This republic was one cunt hair and one religious, dullard vice president away from extinction.

Pence was almost hanged for not being fascist and crazy enough for the base of the Republican Party. By comparison, Barry Goldwater was the Republican presidential nominee in 1964. He was considered at the time to be the most fringe right-wing candidate ever to be nominated. His most famous quotes were "extremism in the defense of liberty is no vice!" and "moderation in the pursuit of justice is no virtue!" Mike Pence is infinitely more to the right of Barry Goldwater, who would be far too liberal to have a place in today's Republican Party. That is how far to the right the party has gone. Pence is anti-abortion, anti-gay rights, and believes in the Dominion Doctrine.

You don't get more conservative than Mike Pence. He literally believes this should be a Christian country and that Christians should be fully in charge. That's what the Dominion Doctrine is. Don't take my word for it. Look it up. They are an **American evangelical Taliban.** And I am very sorry to have to tell you that this is in no way hyperbolic. And Pence is definitely one of them, yet he is not crazy enough for them. No.

Republicans have completely lost control of the monster they themselves created.

Remember we talked about how Republicans know they can't win elections? So what they do is suppress the vote as much as possible. And I'm not kidding. They have passed hundreds of laws across the country making it harder to vote. They have also gone crazy gerrymandering. Yes, it's been going on forever by both parties, but they have gone way past any historical standards.

Then you have the two institutional biases that work for Republicans: The Senate and the Electoral College. I'm not going to make us both crazy by doing a long dialogue about Republican advantages built into the system. The Republicans get twenty senators from ten states that combined have fewer people than the L.A. metro area. That's a pretty big built-in advantage.

Think about that for a second. There are as many people in the Los Angeles metro area as there are in ten **states** combined. Those people in those states get **twenty** senators to represent them. Those people in L.A. get exactly **one**. That alone is a massive advantage and it's just the tip of the iceberg.

Again, I'm not going into this too deep, but Republicans have successfully gerrymandered the states they control so as to radically dilute the power of the Democratic vote. And that too had a role in radicalizing Republicans because so many seats have been gerrymandered into being secure Republican seats. That makes the primaries the only vote that matters to them. So often, Republican primaries become an ongoing race to see who can be the craziest. For the last five years, it has mostly been a battle to see which Republican primary candidate could get their tongue furthest up Trump's bunghole. Almost every national election, Democrats get more overall votes, yet the Republicans end up in the majority.

The Electoral College has also been talked about at length.

Obviously it's not very "democratic" for Trump and W to become president while getting fewer votes than their opponents.

If politics were a metaphor for boxing, Republicans took their gloves off a long time ago. They have become bare-knuckle political brawlers who use every shred of political leverage to retain power, even if that means destroying our Constitution and republic along the way.

They know they can't get the most votes, so the answer is to suppress voting as much as possible. Just think about that sentence for a moment. Much like "flood the zone with shit," suppressing voting is about as un-American as you can get. The whole point of voting is to encourage civic responsibility and participation. By undermining voting, they tear at the very fabric of a democracy.

The bottom line is that they are not playing the game to help the country. They're not even playing the game to actually govern, since they have been preaching anti-government doctrine for forty-five years. They are playing just to win at all costs. Even if one of those costs is our republic. They are specifically playing the game to impose their will against the best interests and desires of the public.

And that's not hyperbole. There are more than enough examples and quotes that demonstrate that they know exactly what they are doing. I'm going to just give you one, and then we will get to the good stuff. This is from the always delightful Mitch McConnell, Senate Majority Leader at the time.

"The single most important thing we want to achieve is for President Obama to be a one-term president."

Now there's a true patriot.

28

THE END OF THE BEGINNING

**"THIS IS NOT THE END. IT IS NOT EVEN THE BEGIN-
NING OF THE END. BUT IT IS, PERHAPS, THE END OF
THE BEGINNING."**

Anybody know who said that? Winston Churchill, on
November 10, 1942. The allies had just won a couple of minor
battles. He knew that the war was still nowhere close to over,
and by no means was victory assured, but he intuitively felt,
correctly, that the tide had finally begun to turn.

I thought that quote was appropriate in that we have spent
quite some time figuring out what has gone wrong. We also
went pretty deep into what it might mean for us to achieve the
goal of a **4 For All** world. We aren't there. We aren't even close.
In fact, it's just as likely that we tumble over into complete
corporate and Republican dominance whose goals are in direct
conflict with the wellbeing of this country. If Republicans win
another election, it may very well be our last.

They have proven that they will stop at nothing and have
even used violence to advance those goals on numerous occasions, the most famous being the January 6th insurrection that

included death and chaos. Yet rather than recoil in disgust, even Republican House members whose lives were in jeopardy on that day have made every effort to downplay its meaning and horror.

But now we know what we want. Now we know what is possible. In short, we know exactly what to ask for. At least we will by the end of this book. I promised you that I have a plan. I do. But it will not be easy. What follows will be an almost step-by-step plan for getting from what the world is now to what it can and should be.

When you have finished with this book, my goal is that you will have a full set of demands that you make of any politician that wants your vote. We want a **4 For All** world. But for now, we are going to work on a **4 For All** United States. Hopefully, we get far enough down that road that we once again become the country the rest of the world wants to imitate. The beacon of light, hope, and freedom, including and especially economic liberty. But first things first. I'm going to spell out **THE EXACT THINGS WE NEED TO ASK FOR.** I promise you, if enough of us get on board we can get it.

Ready, set, go.

PART III

LET'S FIX THIS SHIT

29

CAMPAIGNS, VOTING, CORRUPTION

This is where it all starts. This book started with the notion that there were some questions so important that we don't even know that we should ask them. Here's one: **Why is National Voting Day on Tuesdays?** It's absurd. If you actually want people to vote, why would we vote on a day that almost all of the working people are working? The answer, of course, is that they really don't want people to vote, so they make it harder, so that *fewer* people will vote. **Why do we have to register to vote?** See, I told you some questions are so basic that we don't even think to ask them. If voting is our God-given right and civic responsibility, why in the world would you need to do **ANY FUCKING THING?** You turn eighteen, you are registered. Period. Any form of voter registration is by its very nature voter disenfranchisement. There are no strings attached in the Constitution. Voting is not a privilege, it is a guaranteed right. There should be absolutely no friction in the process whatso-ever. There's a lube joke in here somewhere, but for once I will abstain because it's just that god damn important.

If you want to even pretend to be a patriot, then voting should be made the easiest thing to do. I'll go one step further:

Every eligible voter should be **automatically registered and *required* to vote.** It's literally the only thing we ask of our citizens, participate! And before you object, let me remind you to stay on the fucken planet as it is now. We have the technology for me to get a Roku replacement remote control delivered to my home about two hours after I order it, so we certainly have sufficient technology to create a secure universal voting system.

I'm going to go into this a bit. I envision a world where everyone can simply vote on their phone. You go to the app. It shows you every election you have a vote in. It even allows every candidate to write a couple of paragraphs to present their positions.

So we most certainly have the technology to make a database of every voter everywhere and make sure everyone can and does vote. And if they don't, they will face some nominal fine, like $300,000. Just kidding. Like the equivalent of a parking ticket. That's democracy, that's community, and that's personal responsibility.

So that is the first of our demands. **EVERYONE VOTES AND IT'S VERY, VERY EASY TO VOTE.** When we get to the end, we'll make a handy dandy list of all our demands. For now, we'll go through them item by item.

Of course, Republicans will fight this because they know they can't win if everyone votes. So eventually we will have to make it so that it is in their own best interest to support universal voting. This is how it will be with all of our demands. Enough of us will have to make those demands and eventually the politicians will see that the best way to get elected is to do what us voters say, rather than what the donor class wants. And that brings us to the single most important of all our demands:

CAMPAIGN FINANCE REFORM AND VIGOROUS ANTI-CORRUPTION LAWS BOTH WITH BIG POINTY NASTY TEETH! (IT'S ONLY A LITTLE BUNNY RABBIT.)

Nothing, and I mean nothing, is possible without starting here first. To have any hope of our voices being heard. If there is to be a **4 For All** world, here is where it would have to start. There are a lot of ways to do this, but the one I think would work best for us is a program of **public financing for campaigns**. That is the one that completely levels the playing field to the point where it becomes the politicians' best interest to work for us instead of whoever has the deepest pockets. Remember, the main thing we're looking to accomplish here is to make the politicians *want* and *need* to work for us. We can't expect them to do the right thing from a sense of morality and patriotism. We have to create a system that makes it in their own best interest to do the right things. Align their incentives with our own. Public financing of campaigns, I think, is the best but not the only way to get there.

Along with that, we would need a set of very vigorous anti-corruption laws with very serious repercussions for those who violate them. Again, we are trying to align the politicians' best interest with our own. Which means anti-corruption laws so serious that it simply wouldn't be worth the risk to violate them. Politicians would be forced to run on policies and, if enough of us make our desires clear, they won't dare to run against us. They wouldn't be able to buy their way out of the primaries. And they **can** and **will** say no to the corporate oligarchs. And if they take a single penny, golf trip, or hand job from a special interest, we can lock them up and their public lives would be over. Exactly as it should be.

Impossible, you might be thinking. Not only not impossible but practically automatic if we put the right set of rules in place. Our politicians will work for us once again because it will be in their own self-interest to do so. And what's even better, the quality of the people who will run for public office will gradually, or maybe not so gradually, improve.

Why? Because politics would no longer reward or attract

the mental patients, the power hungry, or those like Mitch McConnell with a for-sale sign pinned to his tiny turtle cock. Public life would be able to attract those with a genuine desire for public service. Again, there are no glory days of electoral perfection to look back on. People have always been people, but we can attract *better* people and those with a genuine desire to help. Because we are designing a system that aligns the politicians' best interests with those of the citizens they are supposed to serve.

This is the first step in the direction of a **4 For All** world. We must enhance voting. We must de-incentivize corruption. And perhaps most importantly, remove money from politics through public financing of elections paired with strict campaign laws. Hard? Yes. Impossible? No.

30

FRAGMENT AND DISPERSE

This is where we finish the work of our Founding Fathers. Where we do the things they would have done could they have ever known it would be necessary. The **ALL MEN ARE CREATED EQUAL** sequel. But let's update it for a world that oddly enough contains some people who are not rich white men. Let's call it the ALL **PEOPLE** ARE CREATED EQUAL SEQUEL. By this I mean that all people are entitled, by birth, to the guarantee of basic existence known as **4 For All**. The granite floor beneath us that frees each of us from fear.

Please note this is **not** the right-wing Republican strawman of taking everything from everybody and redistributing everything until everybody has the exact same thing. Nobody is suggesting **EQUALITY OF OUTCOME**. What **4 For All** will do is assure **EQUALITY OF OPPORTUNITY**. There will always be people with more than other people, and that is just fine and dandy. What we do when we guarantee everyone the basics of life is guarantee equality of opportunity. It unlocks the potential of everyone and will, in the long run, make everybody richer.

There will still be people to look up to and people to look

down on. That is human nature. What there will **not** be is starvation and desperation and a world motivated by fear.

So how do we even begin to fragment and disperse gargantuan economic powers? There are at least two basic and effective tools at our disposal: **massive anti-trust legislation** and **rewriting corporate charters.** Utterly impossible in the world as it is. Completely inevitable in the world of universal voting and a consistent **4 For All** voting coalition.

Oh, and another little thing. It might not be a bad idea if we got corporations to pay some taxes. I spent a couple of days looking at statistics. I went all the way back to 1950. No matter how you slice and dice the stats, one thing is abundantly clear: Corporations pay very, very little compared to historical standards. There is one thing that is not abundantly clear: I'm not sure if they actually pay anything. Once you figure out subsidies and pass through entities and all the other shit, I think net corporate contributions are actually less than zero.

I'm not a hundred percent sure about that, but it's so scarily close to zero as to not matter. I'm going to throw just one stat at you, so you don't glaze over with boredom. In 1950, corporate taxes were equal to almost seven percent of our GDP. Today, it is well less than one percent and possibly a negative number. Dollars and cents, you ask. OK. It means if they paid the same rate now as they did then, corporations would be paying about $1.2 trillion more a year.

I'm sorry, I can't just skip past this because it's absurdly relevant. That difference, over time, is responsible for every last penny of the federal deficit and then some. Bottom line: Corporations outgrew (through regulatory capture) the government's ability to tax them. The problem is not, nor has it ever been, that we spend too much. The problem is that we cannot tax corporations because they control the public officials whose job it is to impose and collect those taxes. It really is just that simple.

And, by the way, when we collect taxes from corporations, it is not largesse. It's not as if they are blessing us with a gift or gesture of good will. Here is that fucker *externalities* again. When we collect taxes from corporations, all we are trying to do is collect enough to offset the externalities of their doing business here.

I know this is a boring and complicated subject, but I beg you to stay with me here. If Wal-Mart pays no taxes, then who pays for the roads that carry their trucks? You. The Navy that protects their shipping lanes? You. The police who arrest their shoplifters and the courts they are tried in? You. Do you get it now? When we ask a corporation to pay taxes, we are not asking for a gift. We are asking them to pay for their share of the infrastructure that we all use, including and especially them. When they overcome government and pay nothing, all that happens is that they are shifting those costs onto the taxpayer . . . you!

That was what Obama was trying to explain when he was famously taken out of context for saying, "You didn't build that." He meant that the infrastructure that makes all business possible is a public good. Republicans, of course, shamelessly piled on to say he was disrespecting the work of plucky small-business owners.

I'm going to beat this dead horse one last time because there is just no way to overstate how important it is, how the corporate ability to evade taxes has changed literally everything for everyone for the much worse. It created an impossible conundrum both for the government and the people it's supposed to serve.

As corporate taxes sunk lower and lower, government was left with an impossible task and an impossible hole to fill. The result was shrinking government service and competence at every level. The deficit swelled even as we slashed, burned, and eventually hallowed out government and its services. Meanwhile, the American working class buckled under the burden because slowly but surely they were the only people left with the means and income to pay taxes but lacked the political clout to avoid them.

The result was the death of the middle class as we knew it and the absurd stratification of wealth. Billionaires and corporations on one side and everybody else on the other.

The trope that government is worthless and incompetent became a self-fulfilling prophecy. The result is a population immersed in fury, distrustful of government, and divided into tribes, each with a list of real grievances. The Republicans were and still are ready to keep digging the hole deeper and doubling down on more tax cuts for corporations and the rich, even as the country and its people come apart at the seams. And they use their right-wing media arm to spread hate and fear. Keeping their victims motivated with hot-button, emotional issues to keep them from seeing the obvious reality that has played out right under their noses.

Look, I could stay at this all day. But I would rather you not kill yourself in despair. We're not dead yet. I'd be lying if I said we weren't close to unsalvageable. But I'd also be lying if I said that there wasn't reason for hope. We can still fix it. That's what we are trying to do right now. Vote **4 For All** for the rest of your life. Tell everyone you know. It can happen. We just have to want it enough. OK, sermon over. Back to work.

Right now, it is every corporation's job to evade taxes because their corporate charter says enhance shareholder value. Not paying taxes certainly furthers that goal. So if they **can** evade taxes, they **must**. And they do. And the rest of us pay the difference. And we are collapsing under the strain.

We talked earlier about rewriting the corporate charter. Remember, right now virtually every corporate charter has similar wording, the point of which is that enhancing shareholder value is their primary reason for existence and the first responsibility of the officers and board of directors. We saw earlier numerous examples of conduct by corporations that, if human, would be considered the actions of an amoral sociopath. The well-documented actions of Nestle, Ford, and every HMO.

Current corporate charters incentivize antisocial behavior in pursuit of profits. Indeed, they **require** it. So let's change it to this:

Enhancing shareholder value is our first priority, but not at the sacrifice of other reasonable priorities. These other priorities include but are not limited to: the wellbeing of all affected by our behavior; our employees, the communities that we serve and wish to serve; and the environment, the earth, and the wellbeing of all who reside here. We will make no attempt to evade reasonable taxation. We will make no attempt to effect political change unless it serves the needs of our corporate stakeholders, which include employees, the communities we serve, the environment, the earth, and our shareholders.

Will this solve every problem? Of course not. But at least it gives corporate leaders a chance to do the right thing even if it doesn't produce immediate gain for the company. At least, in this form, it doesn't **require** them to be assholes. They at least have a choice to behave as something other than amoral shit stains without betraying their fiduciary obligation to shareholders. It's a start.

Next up, it's time to tear down monopolies and duopolies. This is a tricky business because you have two factors to balance when you look at anti-trust. This is not where you go in with an ax and just say "break them all up!" In other words, large is not always synonymous with bad. Economies of scale that large companies provide can be a public good. In other words, sometimes large is best because they have the capital to do giant things that are of benefit to the public and that smaller entities might not be able to accomplish.

For instance, I don't think you go and break up Wal-Mart and Amazon. They are both massive, but they do compete against each other and also other healthy players in the retail space. And customers do get the benefit of their economies of scale and built-out infrastructure and logistics. There might be other reasons not to like them, but size alone isn't one of them. As we talked about earlier, it would be nice if they would pay their employees without taxpayers kicking in five to $8 an hour.

When it comes to "trust busting," the great Theodore Roosevelt said, although not word for word, **too much is better than too little.** The reason he said it and the reason I believe it is that there has not been a single incident where legally breaking up a conglomerate has failed to benefit the consumer and the public good. I couldn't even find an example where an anti-trust action has been bad for the company itself or the entities that resulted from the action. Microsoft was the subject of the last major anti-trust action by the DOJ and, last I checked, they seemed to be OK. The very fact that this case was brought twenty-five years ago tells us that corporate power has remained unchecked for a very long time.

Here's an example that proves the rule. It's also the one that has had the most impact on our lives. AT&T. The original case was brought by the DOJ in 1974 and was finally settled in 1982.

Let's wander about in the green fields of nostalgia for a moment. I am old. But does anyone else remember rotary phones? Do you remember that you couldn't even BUY a telephone?

AT&T's dominance of all telecommunications was so complete that no one even owned the phone in their home. You could only rent it. It always remained company property. I remember what a big deal it was when we could go to a store and buy a phone. And even more impressive, it was soon a push-button phone.

The AT&T settlement resulted in the creation of several regional companies called the "Baby Bells," such as Bell Atlantic and Bell South and others. There could be, and probably are, a bunch of books written about the tidal wave of creativity unleashed by the breakup of this monopoly. But it's safe to say you wouldn't be holding a mini-computer device in your hands right now if it hadn't happened. AT&T as a monopoly had no reason to innovate or change the status quo.

Instead, the new Baby Bells tinkered and innovated. They merged and unmerged with other companies. Some even rejoined AT&T. As they are prone to do, the companies have again merged and congealed down to three main major players in telecommunications: AT&T, Verizon (which came from a couple of the Baby Bells), and T-Mobile, which started as a German company but ended up assembling bits and pieces along the way, including Sprint.

Yes, the power has reassembled, but along the way all of the messy competition brought us wireless communications and incredible advances that simply never would have happened without the breakup. And now with just three real players, it might soon be time to break it up again.

And that's kind of the point of the whole thing. The nature of money, power, and corporations will always be to merge and congeal into bigger and more powerful entities. They will always seek to become a monopoly because, just like in the game of the same name, that is their job. To get everything. Unlimited market power, unlimited pricing power, and unlimited political power.

It is our job as citizens in a democracy to set a fair set of rules and maintain a fair playing field. And to break up power centers when they threaten the public good or become too large or too powerful to regulate.

This is what we cannot do now, at least until we restore voting, discourage and disincentivize corruption, and return our politicians to our own employ. It **can** happen. But it has to start happening now before it's too late. Vote for the vote. Vote for public financing of campaigns. That **must** come first, for everything else to become possible. Including and especially VAT.

31

———

VAT

(AND THE MEANING OF FREEDOM)

Here is another one pulled from the bucket of questions so big that we never seriously think to ask them. Why do we have an income tax in the U.S.? We all just think of it as an inevitable part of life. Income tax is the tax we are thinking of when we say things like "the only thing certain are death and taxes".

But an income tax is not inevitable, nor a given. In fact, the income tax is "celebrating" only its 110th birthday in 2023. María Branyas Morera and a bunch of other living people are older than the United States income tax, as of the writing of this book.

The income tax was incredibly controversial when first proposed early in the twentieth century. It took nothing short of an amendment to the Constitution (the Sixteenth Amendment) to make it legal. One hundred ten years later, we still may not like it, but it seems we have all come to consider income taxes, like death, to be inevitable.

But to me, the income tax is and always will be fatally flawed. Not just because it takes our money (we will get to that soon), but because it takes away our **freedom and rights**, specifically our right to privacy and freedom from government intrusion. Our tax returns give the federal government all the information that we have every right and reason to keep private.

Our tax return reveals:

- What we have
- What we owe
- If we are married
- Who we are married to
- How much we made
- Where we live
- How long we lived there
- What we own
- What we rent
- Where we go
- How we got there
- Where we work
- What we do

I could go on with this all day, but I hope you get the point. While collecting income taxes, the government is privy to virtually every detail of your life. The government knows more about you than most of your friends and family. They probably know more about you than your kids and spouse. How can anyone reconcile this absurd amount of government intrusiveness with any concept of freedom or liberty? I'll give you a hint: You can't. It's ridiculous.

How can you possibly be a **FREE** country and claim to believe in **personal liberty** while your government knows every tiny detail of your financial life? Let's face it, from the information we give them, they know virtually every detail of your private life as well. People who go apeshit when the government encourages them to wear a mask or get a vaccine are oddly OK with spilling their personal and financial guts to that same government every April. Not to mention that the whole process is at gunpoint and the government can toss you in jail if you don't reveal enough information or if you fail to pay the right amount of taxes, which is so complicated that nobody even knows what the right amount is.

The whole concept of income taxes is an abomination and an insult to anyone who genuinely believes in personal freedom and liberty. Plus, the entire tax code is incredibly and ridiculously complex. So complicated that many experts believe that the number of people who file a completely legal and accurate return is **zero**, even if they're trying to. Our tax codes are so chock full of carve-outs and loopholes that even the most learned accountants and lawyers don't know anywhere near all of it.

And that is yet another way that the rich and corporate shift the burden onto the poor and the seventeen people left who are middle class. Its byzantine to the point that the rich can get around it, over it, and through it. It's time to take the entire fucken thing, burn it to the ground, and throw the ashes onto the trash heap of history.

At this point, you have barely been reading the last two or three paragraphs and are still back there wondering why you never thought to question telling the federal government so much intimate information. Come back now so we can talk about how to fix it.

VAT stands for value added tax. But you don't really need to know that because we aren't quite going to use it that way. Think more in terms of a variable national sales tax on goods and services.

For argument's sake, let's say that we want the VAT to produce the same amount of federal revenue as it currently collects from **individual taxpayers** (which is called revenue neutral). It's important to make the distinction because corporations would still be required to pay taxes on earnings. The code for collecting corporate taxes could be simplified and enforced in such a way that they actually start paying taxes.

It's fine and actually desirable to collect information from corporations, even more so if they are privately held as opposed to publicly traded. Public companies are required by the SEC to disclose, whereas private companies are not. So the more we know about privately held companies, the better.

If you just heard a gunshot. That was the Koch brothers paying someone to shoot me. Because the one living brother controls the largest corporate black box in the world. The reason they want to shoot me and the reason they will get away with it are the same. Private companies, even giant, trillion-dollar ones like Koch Industries, can literally get away with murder and disclose almost no information to the public. We know more about the guy who washed your car.

But let's get back to individuals and the VAT. Let me just dress that head wound, hold on a sec. OK. Done. There would be no tax return for any individual, no payroll tax, no nothing. Just a national sales tax that could run from five to thirty percent depending on how progressive you want it to be while remaining revenue neutral (collecting the same amount as we do now). Think of how much time and money is already being saved by avoiding the mountains of paperwork you, and your employer have to deal with now.

We would have the ability to make the VAT style tax next to nothing on consumer staples and healthcare, but up to thirty or forty percent for luxury goods and services. There's a million ways to do this right and, even if we fuck it up, it would still be better than what we have now. Today we spend billions on a system no one can understand that requires us to take our pants down for the federal government. A VAT would be simple, fair, and progressive by nature and even more so if we want it to be.

The best part? We get to restore our freedom and privacy. You don't even have to wear a mask.

Just add it to the list of demands you make of anyone who wants your vote. Don't worry. You don't have to keep track. There will be a list of your demands at the end.

32

———

EDUCATION

(WITH PUBLIC AND CIVIL RESPONSIBILITY)

Democracy requires knowledgeable citizens, and an economy requires skilled workers. Yes, a **4 For All** world will still need skilled workers. So here is how we do it. Right now, K-12 school is considered a public good and is paid for publicly. That worked just fine for the agrarian society of 1776. Not so much for today. In the twenty-first century, we have to do it a little differently than we did when we were essentially training ranch hands.

All **K-PhD** is considered a public good and is paid for publicly. Everyone is expected to finish high school at grade twelve. Those who wish to go on and have the aptitude will continue up to and including graduate school. Yes, that includes medical, legal, and dental schools all paid for publicly.

We have another path for those that finish high school that don't want to go or are not qualified to move on to college. There will be publicly funded trade and technical schools for those who wish to attend. All also publicly funded.

Let me piss you off just a bit more before you start yelling about how we can't afford to do this. We would also require two years of public service from all graduates beginning when they complete their field of studies. There could be some flexibility to the program where a student could complete their two years of public service and then return to continue in their course of study. There will be numerous types of public service available, but some would be dictated by the field of study.

Specialized graduates in the medical or legal fields would do public service related to those fields. For instance, a newly minted doctor might spend two years in an underserved region. A newly minted lawyer would do two years of *pro bono* work or as a public defender or assistant public prosecutor.

For more general study graduates, there would be choices including the military or various forms of civil service. No one would be forced into the military, but all would be required to do those two years of civil service. Types of services could include an updated version of the Peace Corps, assistance for the elderly, environmental clean-ups. The possibilities are endless, but all would produce one public good that we now sorely lack: social and civic cohesion with a sense of community.

We would educate all our children to the best of **their** ability. In return they would give us two years of service.

I know this is a big leap, but just give yourself some time to consider how vast the benefits would be.

And the costs are much less than you might think. I looked at this from several different angles and ran the numbers in several different ways. And most of what I found suggested that the long-term benefits would produce an ROI (return on investment) of close to or actually **exceeding** initial costs.

The benefits ultimately would far, far exceed the costs in some ways that are obvious and others that are harder to quantify but no less important. Consider the value of getting the best that each of us has to give and unlocking the vast potential of people who might not otherwise have that chance. Consider the value of civic engagement and a shared sense of community. Consider the value of fully educated, motivated, and confident young people.

We will have a virtual army of motivated young people armed with the skills and knowledge to achieve what they **want** to do, not what financial circumstances forced upon them. Can you think of a better definition of freedom and liberty than this?

Think of our national interest. In a few years, we would have the best-prepared and best-trained workforce in the world by far. That's not just an economic benefit but a civic and national security benefit as well.

Now imagine the economic stimulus of educated and motivated young people returning from their two years of public service. All brimming with training, world experience, and not saddled in debt.

But the single most important benefit is this: Imagine being an American born into a world that you know will give you every avenue to reach your full worth. Your fullest potential. This value alone is beyond money. Practically beyond imagination.

Will every kid turn out great? Of course not. But at least every child will have the chance, a damn good chance at that. Priceless, but free. Or so close to it as not to matter.

4 For Fucken ALL!

33

BUILD, BUILD, BUILD!!!
(AND WHEN YOU ARE DONE BUILDING, BUILD SOME MORE.)

We talked earlier about the reason that housing has become a crisis-level problem in the United States.

There are several underlying reasons that can be addressed, but all of them have the same cure. Build. One of the big issues is that we printed a whole lot of money just before and during the pandemic. All but four percent of it went to corporations in one form or another. The four percent was those $600 checks you got.

I'm going to use a very conservative figure of $4 trillion as the amount that we printed and gave to corporations. The people who actually hold the shares of those companies are mostly **not** Americans. So think about this. We printed $4 trillion (actually more) and handed out the largest part of it to foreign investors.

There is a huge amount of evidence to suggest that many of these entities used that money to buy up U.S. real estate as safe haven for our largesse. That caused real estate prices and rents to spike to the highest levels in history. So to put it bluntly, we are now paying outrageous rents to foreign owners of land and real estate that used to be ours. If that doesn't make you sick to your stomach, it should.

Real estate was always and almost mythically a big part of the American Dream. That dream is now out of reach for the vast majority of Americans. Real wages already weren't keeping up with rent and real estate values. The events around the pandemic seemed to have put the last nail in the coffin. Two generations are virtually locked out of home ownership and with that, almost any hope of financial security, never mind retiring one day. Don't ask me which generations because I get confused with X, Y, Z, and Alpha and the Millennials. I'm either a Boomer or an X depending on whose definition you use. No matter what you call them, they're screwed.

Because of scarcity, housing has become two things that it's not really intended to be: storehouses of generational wealth and casinos, rife with speculation like players at the roulette wheel.

The good news is that all these questions have the same answer: Build. Build and keep building until housing is housing. It can also still be a storehouse of value, but we must build so much that we change the perception of housing from being an investment back to being the place you **live in** and **own**.

Here's the **4 For All** answer. First, change laws so that only **individuals** can own **residential** real estate. It makes perfect sense. A corporation is not a person. It does not require a physical "home." It may require office space on commercial property, but definitely not a "home." So they should have no business in residential real estate. But people do. And while we are at it, let's limit how many residences a single individual can own. Let's make it a perfectly reasonable number, like five. A rich person can personally own up to five dwellings for their personal use. A person may rent their dwelling to other people. But a corporation cannot own them nor rent them out. That won't completely stop speculation, but it will make it much harder.

When it comes to existing rental complexes owned by corporations, those properties can and must lawfully pass to individual owners of each unit. The government can assist in the transition at a relatively modest cost, with financial assistance and cheap loans for renters to acquire the units they live in.

People take care of things they own. They shit on things they rent. That is human nature, and no amount of money will change that. So here comes the good part.

The federal government will build roughly **forty million new units** spread throughout the country. This will cost anywhere between $2 trillion and $4 trillion depending on where you build and whose numbers you use. Don't even fucken bother to tell me we can't afford that. This chapter started with us simply printing and giving away more money than solving the housing crisis will cost. So just cut the shit!

We are going to build until scarcity is a thing of the past.

The government will not be giving these new units away but will provide cheap loans and incentives that can vary by region. Look, I'm not delusional. There are inner city and suburban areas where building will be impractical or impossible. So it will be necessary to think creatively. In some cases, it will mean establishing all-new towns. We can do it. If China can do it, if Dubai can do it, we can fucken do it!

Much of the cost of these new projects will be reclaimed over the short and long haul. The government will sell them at somewhere around cost, but there are dozens of virtuous but hard to quantify benefits. This includes the jobs that will be created in building these homes.

I can't promise that we will reclaim every dollar spent on this effort, but even if it only amounts to sixty-five percent, which is the lowest of the predicted possibilities. It would still far and away be the best and highest use of tax dollars. The benefits are so many and so widespread as to be incalculable. And there are some reasons to believe that the government may eventually do better than break even on the proposition. But even if it doesn't, it's still more than worth doing.

It's time for this country to think big again. We used to do it. We can do it. Once we regain control of our political system, we **must** do it. All of us can have a piece of the American Dream. We just have to want it. We just have to vote for it.

And this would go hand in hand with . . .

A MASSIVE PUBLIC WORKS PROGRAM TO REBUILD AND MODERNIZE OUR CRUMBLING INFRASTRUCTURE

As long as we are already building new housing throughout the country, let's make a simultaneous effort to rebuild our current, crumbling infrastructure. Let's build roads, fix bridges, strengthen our electrical grid, work toward greener solutions, and climate-change-proof as much of the country as we can. Let us all put at least as much effort into this as we do cursing at strangers on the internet. These things aren't impossible. They are not even improbable. We crushed Nazis! We went to the fucken moon for Christ's sake! Greatness is our legacy as a people. All we have to do is get our politicians working for us again.

I know. It's been a long, slow, and steady decline. Lots of us were born into a world that was already under complete corporate control of our lives. So they don't have memory of anything else. They are told government is their enemy and utterly impotent. And the world today offers them no evidence to believe otherwise. But many of us can remember a strong, confident, and bold America that did huge, great things for our own country and for others. Yes, we did some stupid things too, but the good always far eclipsed the ill-conceived or overconfident. The greatness is still there, just below the surface. We can once again be the beacon of all that is good, we just have to want it.

We are, almost all of us, patriots. And as corny as it may sound, what we seem to have lost, more than anything else, is **pride.** Yes, we all go through the motions and we have twenty-six holidays to honor our veterans. But you walk into a post office, and you might as well have gotten off the bus in Beirut. Spiritless, dead-eyed people behind the counter going through the motions. They too are the victims of a half a century of degradation and neglect. Or more recently with Trump, outright contempt. If you are truly a patriot, how can you bear to see your shabby post office? Your disgusting DMV? Do you love and stand for your flag? Then love and care for your country. Or else you are just a poser. Going through the motions of patriotism. Signaling for meaningless virtue.

That is why the right-wing politics since Reagan are so insidious and corrosive. Think about it for a second. If we are supposed to be a democracy, then what are you really saying when you say that government is bad, incompetent, untrustworthy, or worse? You are saying that **we as a people** are bad because government is a reflection of the people. At least it's supposed to be. So we can wrap ourselves in the flag, wear it as a tie pin, and pledge allegiance all day long, but don't fucken pretend that makes you a patriot. Because when you say that government, by nature, is bad, you are saying that we, as a people, are bad. There is just no way around it. In a democracy, if your government is bad, it is YOUR FUCKEN JOB TO FIX IT!

So we will. **4 For All!**

34

HEALTHCARE

(WITHOUT THE QUESTION MARK)

Now it's time to talk about healthcare. Not the business of healthcare. Actual healthcare.

There is really no debate to be had here. People are not stupid, and they can feel it when you stick something in their ass. Some find it a convenient place to keep their car keys, but hey, to each their own. We want a single-payer healthcare system, no matter how many different times or ways the question is asked. This has been true for as long as polling has existed. Quick numbers:

In 2020, more than $4 trillion was spent on healthcare in the U.S. That represents a truly astounding 17.7 percent of our GDP. (GDP is the complete total of all the goods and services in the whole country.) Healthcare's share has been steadily rising as a percentage of GDP at about half a percent a year. You don't have to be a genius to know this is not working and is unsustainable and getting worse all the time.

I don't care how much you have been trained like a seal to hate the government, yourself, and what you completely misunderstand as being socialist, you know you are being screwed. Sometimes you take a splinter out of a dog's paw and the motherfucker bites you for your trouble. Fine. Bite away. But **Medicare for All** is far and away our best choice.

There are enough reasons to fill several volumes, but I will give you but two. First, much of the infrastructure is already in place with Medicare, so the transition to that single-payer system can be relatively smooth. Second, even if the government lives up to Ronald Reagan's worst expectations, it is still guaranteed to be much better and cheaper than what we have now. By a lot.

The absolute highest cost estimates of Medicare for All come in at about $3 trillion a year. That was the highest estimate. So even if it lives up to our absolute worst fears and expectations, we the people are already saving $1 trillion a year. Folks, it's not even close. If it does just a pretty shitty job, we can expect to save a couple trillion a year. Plus, everyone is covered. Nobody lives in constant fear of financial ruin if they get sick. And tons of people will not get expensive deadly diseases because they won't be financially afraid of going to the doctor. That alone will save us a ton of money. This is a complete and total no-brainer.

Doctors will love it because it will free them from mountains of unnecessary paperwork. Businesses will love it because they can get themselves out of the healthcare business and concentrate on what their actual business is. Patients will love it because there will be a single set of known rules and they will know exactly who to talk to if they have a question or if something goes wrong. Everyone will end up paying less than they pay now.

The only people who won't like it are the same people that have been able to keep us from getting it. The people who make billions by preventing us from getting the care we need: HMOs. They are nothing more than organized crime. Hostage takers. People who stand between you and your doctor, taking a piece of both of you. Are you starting to get the sense that I don't particularly care for these ruthless, monstrous, bloodsucking pieces of shit?

I know. It's impossible now. The HMOs take our money and use it to own our politicians and our democracy. I get it. Let this be the reason that motivates you to put on that **4 For All** T-shirt. Let this be the reason that gets you on board, voting to get the universal frictionless voting and campaign finance reform that will restore our democracy. It is truly a matter of life and death. For you, me, our democracy, our country, and even the people who have been brainwashed into MAGA and hopelessness.

We can do it. We must do it.

DRUGS

What kind of legal and illegal drug policy is compatible with the **4 For All** world that we are going to create? Before we begin, let's go with the obvious. Mass marketing and television advertising for prescription drugs is ridiculous and has to go. But we can't go too far. There is some public good in marketing new and novel approaches. I suspect that it could be worked into the FDA process for approving drugs. When a new drug is reviewed and approved for public use, the FDA could provide public service announcements to raise public awareness. They could also make physicians aware of new treatments and therapies through direct communication with the medical community.

The one thing we don't need is what we have now. The armies of briefcase-dragging prostitutes roaming the country and preying on (and sucking on) doctors. Endless commercials on television about toe fungus. Drug manufacturers would need to dismantle their marketing arm. The irony is that they will scream at the top of their lungs at first, but they would almost certainly benefit in the long run by not needing to spend tens of millions of dollars on marketing. If a drug works, it will sell. Without being whored out.

Ironic side note: In 1971, it became illegal to advertise cigarettes on television and radio. Predictably, the companies cried bloody murder and fought the restrictions tooth and nail. But the result was absolutely no decrease in sales and an actual benefit to their bottom line. I suspect a similar result once we stop drug companies from running commercials for a drug that helps you straighten out your bent penis. There are times that I wish I was just making things up. I am, after all, primarily a fiction writer. But I am sorry to say that I am not making this up. Drug companies gave a name to the condition of having a bent penis (Peyronie's disease) and then starting selling a cure for it. Excuse me, I meant a *treatment* for it. We already know that there isn't money in curing things.

So let's start with the reasonable proposition that many of the things that stoke substance abuse would not be factors in a **4 For All** world. The pressures and fears of our current life would be far reduced. So there would be fewer reasons to want to use mood-altering substances to escape the new reality we would create.

But it would also be naïve to think that the problem would vanish. Alcohol use is almost as old as civilization itself. Marijuana is now mostly an acceptable part of our lives and society. I would suggest that we focus our efforts on the handful of illegal drugs that do almost all of the damage. At the moment, we are talking about fentanyl (an incredibly powerful and addictive synthetic opioid), crystal methamphetamine, and Xylazine (aka "Tranq," a horse tranquilizer).

Nostalgia alert: When I was a kid, my parents, like most parents, warned me against the use of illegal drugs. The popular approach of the time was to tell children that all drugs will immediately kill you and cause one of your testicles to drop out and roll across *Queens Boulevard*. You will then die again as you race carelessly across the street, in chase of your lost and still rolling testicle. Ok, it wasn't quite that severe. But they really did say that every illegal drug would kill you or make you lose your mind so that you might jump off a building thinking you could fly. The real problem with this approach was that they painted every drug with the same brush, so that when my friends and I started smoking weed we didn't believe our parents anymore. Nobody died. Nobody went crazy. Some of us ate a lot of Chinese food and went to sleep. Others stayed up and called overnight TV evangelist preachers and promised to make large donations in the names of people they didn't like or names they made up. Willie Phistergach and Hugh Gassole were very frequent donors. The point is that our parents lost credibility. And if they were wrong about weed, what else were they wrong about? So, many of us went on to dabble in things that really could hurt us. Acid, mescaline, quaaludes (a prescription barbiturate), black beauties (a form of meth), and a bunch of other shit that was readily available and fucked up a lot of us.

But in the current world, the illegal drugs **really** are every bit as bad as the ones our parents warned us about. The big three at the moment are opioids (fentanyl, heroin, etc.), *crystal methamphetamine* and a horse tranquilizer called *xylazine* (tranq). Or some combination of the three. And people are dying from abuse at levels never seen before. It is nothing short of a deadly crisis. Part of the problem is that fentanyl is ridiculously powerful but also very cheap to synthesize. So dealers add it to EVERYTHING like it's salt and pepper. And if their calculations are off by even the tiniest bit, they kill their customers. It's happening everywhere. Dealers are even adding fentanyl to drugs like cocaine so that people are getting addicted to fentanyl without ever knowing that they took it. The world my parents lied to me about back then really does exist now. This shit will addict you and kill you with a quickness.

This isn't going to go away anytime soon. Even with the magic wand of **4 For All**. So I would suggest that we focus our resources on the most dangerous drugs and make everything else completely legal. Even benzos, weed, and cocaine. This way we can use all of our resources to fight the true dangers and change the focus of enforcement from incarceration to education and treatment. Putting these people in jail accomplishes nothing except costing us money. Plus, it ends up being just another way for them to network with each other to buy, sell, and use more drugs. Unless you want to just kill them and get it over with? No, I didn't think so. So let's concentrate on education and treatment. Make sure everyone knows how deadly this shit is and focus on treating those that are already deadly seriously addicted. It's cold to say but absolutely true. This epidemic will end itself soon enough *by itself*. By killing most, if not all of its victims. And when that happens there will almost always be a new set of substances waiting in the wings.

In our new 4 **For All** world, we will need to remain vigilant, limber, and responsive. Again, legalize all but the deadly drugs and be ready to focus our enforcement efforts on education, diversion, and treatment. Taxes on the legalized drugs will help to fund our efforts to fight deadly drugs and help society to recoup the *externalities* of their use.

Even in our 4 **For All** heaven, there will still be a few junkies. But with our politicians working for us, we can minimize the damage to the users and the country.

35

UTILITIES

(WHAT IS, WHAT ISN'T)

When you think of the word "utilities," the first thing that springs to mind is usually your electric company. Maybe your water or trash collection. When I started doing research for this section, I came across definitions of utilities that included way more than I expected, like transportation, mail services, education, and telecommunications. But for the purpose of this discussion let's think of utilities as being the things we all need and can't do without. Let's narrow it down to:

- Water (including sewer and waste disposal)
- Power (home electric and gas service)
- Home internet
- Postal service

There are other things that could have gone on this list that are very important, but can work pretty well as part of free enterprise and free markets.

I believe strongly that water and power must be owned and operated publicly. Water and power you absolutely must have. You will not die without internet but it's not all that far off. I was tempted to put wireless communications on this list. But ultimately I believe it can be left to a lightly regulated free market.

We are pretty much down to just three major wireless providers. But there is still ample competition. We cannot permit that market to consolidate any further. The last major merger was the deal between Sprint and T-Mobile. The story of that merger was practically a crash course in the modern corruption that I have been bitching about on every page of this book. Eighty-six members of the U.S. House of Representatives signed a letter to the FCC and DOJ **in favor** of the merger. Claiming, absurdly, that it would bring increased competition and lower prices for consumers. Not a single economist or human with an IQ over thirty-seven agreed with them. And of course it had the exact opposite effect. Wireless prices, which had been steadily dropping for the prior decade stabilized and then started going up. Surprise!! Fun fact: every whore, excuse me, every U.S. House member who signed that letter was on the payroll of both *Sprint* and *T-Mobile* and even *Verizon*. All had received campaign donations from the companies. It's like they don't even bother to try to hide it anymore. They are openly and proudly corrupt.

I won't take credit for this concept. It might have been Robin Williams who said that politicians should be like Nascar drivers and have to wear the logos of the companies that they work for.

And this is why we can't afford to fuck around anymore with the basics of life. You ready?

Nationalize every private fucken electric, gas, and water utility in the country. That is far and away the most radical thing said in this book. It will cause a shit storm and that's OK. But once we are back in control of our government, it will be time to take away their ATMs. We the people cannot afford to be held hostage by increasingly foreign-owned entities that control the levers of our basic fucken existence.

We will publicly own every electric, water, and gas utility, and if they don't watch their step, we will nationalize the two shit-stain ISPs (internet service providers) as well. If we are going to leave home internet service as part of the free market, then we are going to have to arrange to have at least one or more new competitors for AT&T and Comcast. And even that won't completely fix it. There must be strict price controls in place for any location that has less than two ISP choices. Right now that is virtually the entire country.

As for the mail, the United States Postal Service used to be the envy of the entire world. Fed Ex, UPS, and others have used their financial powers to use Congress to gut this former symbol of our national pride. This is not the worst example of disgusting corruption in this book. But it bothers me more than most. Maybe it's because the postal service is one of the most visible signs of our decline as a nation under the thumb of oligarchy. But it also might be that I am the grandson of an incredibly proud **union** postal worker. Maybe it's because I saw and felt his pride about what he did for a living and the people he served.

It is well past time for us to restore our pride and patriotism. It is well past time to restore this symbol of our nation to its former greatness. My research revealed that the USPS more than pays for itself when it is not intentionally handicapped by a shamefully bought and paid for Congress. And if for no other reason, support them out of self-interest. If you live outside of any major city you will pay much, much more to mail a letter if the USPS goes the way of the buffalo.

36

GUNS

(IN A 4 FOR ALL WORLD)

If you have gotten this far in this book then it's likely that you know where I stand on guns. They hold a unique place in the history of our nation and a pretty notorious place in its decline and submersion into the swamp of corruption.

There's also nothing that can be said or done to change my mind that the primary purpose for owning a gun is to buttress and support the painfully frail male ego. The younger and weaker the man, the bigger the need for the gun, and the bigger the gun itself. We have seen this time after time. Bloody massacre after bloody massacre.

With all of that said, I am **not** in support of a total gun ban in this **4 For All** world that we will create. We won our independence with an armed citizen army, and because of that, firearms are practically a part of our DNA. That makes my own personal opinion on the matter irrelevant. And in that area, just so you know, even I would not support a sweeping ban of firearms in the United States.

But we do have to do something, and that something would be in two parts.

Ban guns that have no legitimate use other than to kill

people. I can't give you a list. Despite some knowledge gained from writing a novel about a sniper, I am far from knowledge-able when it comes to firearms.

At the same time, I am sure that once the government is in **our** employ, rather than the employ of the **NRA**, something can be worked out.

It is also time for the industry and its customers to pay their own bills. Taxpayers and voters in a **4 For All** world will not stand for continuing to pay a public price for their private fun and frailty of ego.

I would suggest taxing the weapons themselves, as well as the ammunition. Gun folks, of course, will lose whatever is left of their minds. But it's a no-brainer. Why would anyone ever think it's OK that the taxpayers should be stuck paying for what is essentially someone else's entertainment and emotional crutch? This "right" costs us all dearly in blood and money. We wouldn't and don't stand for it on any other subject.

I'm not going to repeat all the horrors of guns and corruption that we discussed at length earlier. We know that recovering external costs of private transactions is a big part of a functioning free market democracy. They can still have their guns. But they must pay their true costs. Fair is fair.

PART IV

FROM HERE TO THERE

First things first. We didn't get where we are overnight. The dilemma we find ourselves in now took shape over decades. It was, in essence, a slow-motion coup. Little by little, year by year, the corporate power structure chipped away at our national sovereignty and democracy. Now, we are not so slowly being looted by corporations that have no natural or national allegiance to the United States. They serve only their shareholders, whom at this point are mostly foreigners or might as well be because they cannot and do not hold dear this country nor its people.

Caring for this country and its people is not their job. It's our job. And we have to start doing it before it is too late. Time is running out. What follows is an almost step-by-step plan for rebuilding American democracy and sovereignty. The first three steps are the hardest, but also the most important.

- **Publicly Funded Elections**
- **Universal and Frictionless Mandatory Voting**

- **Very Strong and Fully Enforced Anti-Corruption Law**

Without these three, nothing else on the list below will be possible. So our immediate demands of every politician must be for these three things. Easy? Fuck no! Possible? Yes. But we must be steadfast in these demands and create an active voting block of **4 For All** supporters. These three demands are those of the **real patriots** of true American democracy, liberty, and sovereignty. And we must not be afraid to say so, over and over again until we are heard. Vote for it as if your life, and the lives of your children, depend on it. Because that is the truth.

All the rest of this becomes real and possible once we have regained our freedom.

- Changing the corporate charter
- Anti-trust action and legislation
- Pierce the corporate veil (hold corporate executives criminally liable)
- Proper and fair taxation of corporations
- VAT tax (to replace income tax for individuals)
- Huge penalty for employing illegal workers
- Reform of legal immigration laws
- Medicare for All
- K-PHD publicly funded education
- Publicly funded technical and occupational training
- Two years civil/military service
- Prioritize and subsidize scaling of lab-grown meat
- Build forty million new dwellings
- Only individuals can own residential real estate
- Nationalize public utilities
- Regulation and/or competition for ISPs
- Regulation and/or competition for wireless providers

- Outlaw private prisons
- Legalize all drugs except opioids, crystal meth, and "Tranq" (for now)
- Divert enforcement funds to treatment and education

Oh yeah, I almost forgot. **Tax** the child-molesting, free-loading, soul-stealing churches. Was that a bit harsh? Let me try again. **Tax** the mother-fucking-delusional pieces of shit and their invisible, white sky daddy! Hold on, give me one more try. Let's tax churches. It makes no sense for taxpayers to subsidize anyone's beliefs. They are free to have insipid, harmful, and ignorant beliefs. But there is nothing in the Constitution that says that the rest of us have to pay for it.

There are two things absent from this list that you might think are necessary to create the **4 For All** world. Direct public assistance and minimum wage laws. There is a reason they have been left off. If everything else on this list is accomplished, we will not need a minimum wage law, and public assistance would remain at current levels or perhaps even less than we spend now.

The immigration changes and penalties for employing illegal workers will create a true free market for labor. Wages will rise naturally as they won't be artificially suppressed as they are now. So it is very unlikely that any sort of minimum wage would be necessary. And if necessary it can be approached from a different direction. Right now, the taxpayer subsidizes low-wage workers with the employer pocketing the difference. That in itself is a form of corporate socialism. Instead, we require the companies themselves to make up the difference in paying their employees a living wage. Although I suspect that this might not even be necessary.

With the changes above, it is likely that there will be little need for direct public assistance. Yes, there will always be those that fall behind for any number of reasons. The disabled and handicapped must be cared for under any economic system and the **4 For All** world will be no different. But on the level playing field that we are creating, very few will be left behind. The vast majority will fare just fine without economic help. Because they will have something much better than monetary help. They will have real **economic opportunity**.

37

FRUSTRATION = MOTIVATION

Our failure to tax corporations for half a century has created a giant hole in our economy that cannot be filled by taxpayers or the continuous degradation of government and the services and infrastructure it provides. The hole has grown bigger and bigger over the last forty years, even as the middle class buckles under the strain and government receded. Even as our government has grown less competent and even less able to grasp the issues, let alone work to correct them, they fight amongst themselves at the fringes without the slightest notice or care for the systemic corruption at the heart of its intentional dysfunction. That dysfunction serves only vast economic interests. As we know, nature abhors a vacuum. Corporate power is all too happy to fill the void left as our democracy decays.

It's frustrating. It's beyond frustrating. The answers are so clear and simple and yet so far from our grasp. We know enough to know what to do, yet we still can't get anywhere close. In fact, we get further and further away with every passing moment. And I can't even blame us for throwing up our hands in hopelessness.

And corporate media keeps us fighting with ourselves so

that we won't notice them. They use glittery (although still important) social and racial issues to keep us busy as they back up the truck and make off with our money and democracy. They have flooded the zone with shit and taken away our sense of reality and a common set of facts to work with. This has produced a toxic stew of apathy and anger for one another. Exactly as intended.

I can't tell you that every answer I've given is the right one, but I will swear with my last breath that the **first three items are one hundred percent correct** and will open our opportunity to make real changes. Without those three massive changes, we have no hope.

Now is the point where I tell you that I am extremely handsome man, a snazzy dresser, a great dancer and that I am 100% right about the entire list below the three absolutely crucial first steps. But the truth is that I can't dance, nor can I guarantee that the list of actions above are the only surefire way to bring about a **4 For All** world. But it's a damn good place to start. Once we have control over our government again, a whole new world will open up to us. Are we going to fuck up sometimes? Sure! Is the government going to fuck up sometimes? Absolutely! But when we fail, it will be together and in pursuit of the greater good for our country and its people. Not the shortsighted gains of the looting foreign investors and hedge funds that care nothing for our wellbeing.

This will be the last of our thought experiments. If you needed a serious surgery, which of these surgeons would you choose? A decent, well-meaning doctor with average surgical skills (government), or a first-in-his-class genius whose only interest in you is dollar signs and producing as much income from your illness as possible (corporate)?

And even that is not a fair analogy. Americans have been conditioned to believe that large private industry is more efficient than government, especially this depleted, atrophied version of government we are currently stuck with. But it's not true, even in the abstract, and even less true when you consider the purpose of corporate efficiency. The purpose of private industry is to provide shareholder value and profit. If their ice cream is cold and yummy or you survive the surgery of the corporate doctor. Even then it is only a performative and ancillary product of their real goal. They can't and don't give two shits if your ice cream is yummy or if you are alive to eat it. They can only care about profiting from it.

There will be criticism of the goals stated here. I can already hear the cries of "Big Government!" But when I hear "Big Government," what I hear is big **"we the people."** We can't get by on rugged independence, and the truth is we never did. The people who think that way are delusional and longing for a world that never existed in the first place. Humans are social animals, and if you want to go it alone, you have every right to expect the life expectancy of the middle ages. None of us can produce all of the things we need to live. And the few who think so may very well be skilled gardeners and builders, but their real talent is self-delusion and cognitive dissonance.

Technology has advanced and the world has become more complex and crowded. And there is no "frontier" to escape to and go it alone. Interdependency is the reality of a rationally lived life, whether we care to admit it or not. One of the greatest ironies in a book overflowing with them is this: The people who cry the most about government interfering in their lives are the ones that depend on it the most. Remember the guy at the Trump rally who belligerently growled to the camera, "Keep your god damn government hands off my Medicare." You can't make this shit up—it writes itself. The red states with the strongest resentment toward the government also rely heavily on it, as well as on the financial support from the blue states, which contribute significantly more to the federal treasury. The much hated and maligned liberal California is by itself the fifth-largest economy in the world. Not too bad for a bunch of socialists.

The government will do just fine once they are working for us and closely watched with plenty of guardrails in place. So yes, all of this shit is incredibly frustrating. But the truth is there will be an ending to this ridiculous dysfunction and systemic absurdity one way or another.

It can really only go one of two ways. The Republicans win a national election. They use that power to continue and intensify disenfranchisement and change state and national laws to the point where they can never lose again. At that point, there will be no further meaningful voting in the United States. The American experiment will be at an end. Completely unleashed, corporations will cut off the last of the air to our democracy. The result will be much like what we have seen the last forty years, but supersized. The United States, already declining on the world stage, will march quickly toward economic and political impotence. Millions more will be imprisoned as protest, homelessness, and starvation are criminalized, as is already beginning to happen. With its still vast military, it may very well be the U.S. that begins a massive world confrontation in a desperate attempt to remain relevant and to secure resources.

This scenario, sadly, appears to be the most likely at the moment. But out of that chaos and war will eventually grow a resistance. It is simply the way of things. It may take decades, but eventually there will be an overthrow of one-party rule. Most likely a violent overthrow. This of course assumes that there still remains a country and a world, which is by no means certain. There are already stirrings among the young that have lost faith in capitalism and have more than a metaphoric desire to "eat the rich."

But eating the rich is not necessary nor desirable. This would be a hard case to make for the young people saddled by debt and working three jobs to eke out a living, just to be told by Boomers to "skip the avocado toast." But I'm going to make the case anyway.

The billionaires of this world are as victimized by our corruption as the rest of us, albeit quite a bit more comfortably. Does a single fucken billionaire you've ever seen look happy? I've personally met several and observed dozens more. They are no happier than the rest of us. Perhaps even less so. It would be presumptuous for me to say that they know that they undeservingly live lavish lives at the expense of millions of hard-working people, yet I think they do know, at least at some level. Undeservingly? Fuck yes. No one human being deserves or can be trusted with wealth of this magnitude.

Of course, people deserve to enjoy the fruits of their work or innovation, but not on this scale. It is simply "unnatural," as such prominence and affluence exists among no other species. And every single one of them will suffer and die just as we do. They will suffer heartbreaks and pain no different than us. Perhaps, at times, even worse. Steve Jobs killed himself through his arrogance of affluence and power. Elon Musk was recently quoted in an interview saying that *death would be a relief*. He is not a happy man nor is he a stupid one. He knows he is a fraud. He knows he is a scion of power and wealth and an usurper of the accomplishments and glory of many others. He is a miserable man speaking the words I would sooner expect to hear from a black-lunged coal miner. Can you remember a single member of Britain's royal family that ever appeared to be happy? Our own version of royalty, the Kennedys, have a well-documented history of misery, family tragedy, and substance abuse.

The men who signed the Declaration of Independence were all very rich and accomplished. They were all among the richest and most powerful people alive at the time. Together they created the greatest country ever known. But even the poorest of the modern billionaires are many magnitudes richer and more powerful than *all of them combined.* Humans were just not designed to wield this level of power and influence. A lone tyrant can be killed and eaten and his power dispersed. No such solution exists for the power of incomprehensible wealth. It is a force independent of its "owner." For all their money and power, I think they are as powerless as the rest of us. They are the benefactors of this corruption but not its master. They will all age. They will all die. And they can give every penny away to charities without putting a dent in the systemic problems that have metastasized over our lives and our country.

No, there is no reason to "eat the rich," which of course is just a metaphor for the violent overthrow of capitalism and oligarchy. There is the second option of our two possible outcomes: political reforms which restore our democracy while restoring our liberties and the fundamental value of capitalism. Yes, **4 For All.**

We started with the notion that the world has more than enough resources for everyone. This is truth. But being true doesn't make it happen. That is *our* job. This is a form of morality that we all have at the center of our spirit. Almost everyone would actually vote to "flip the switch" if they only understood that it was possible. Well, now you do. What are you going to do about it? That's where motivation comes in.

Start by trying to imagine a **4 For All** world. Imagine the genuine freedom it would bring. Imagine the fear draining from our lives. Imagine families that can stay near each other if they choose to. Imagine living every waking moment with your economic survival assured. Imagine every relationship in life being one of choice rather than necessity. Imagine the peace that would settle upon us all.

I know, I speak of magic. I'm embarrassing myself. Trust me, it's not the first time. But it's real and it's possible. But first we have to KNOW it's possible and BELIEVE and make everyone around you believe. Then we can act. We can vote only for those who understand and believe. Expect and demand from every public official exactly what we want. Freedom. Not freedom to work, starve, and worry. No, real freedom. Real liberty for everyone.

No one politician can make it happen alone. That's why we must know and share all of these goals. Then we can ask every politician that wants our vote exactly what part they intend to play in the creation of the **4 For All** world

I'm not talking about a spiritual manifestation, unless that's what you want to call imagination. Because at the end of the day they are practically one and the same. You can't make anything happen unless you can envision it first. Know it. See it. Believe it. And make it happen.

The alternative is not just more of the same. In case you haven't been paying attention, the wheels are falling off quickly. The window is closing on our country and our species. Look around you. Unless you are already at least a millionaire, you and most of the people you know are struggling. People have stopped having children simply because they cannot afford them. More than half the population is between one and three missed paychecks away from homelessness or worse. All of us are struggling and about a third of us have been unredeemably brainwashed. *We the people* are drowning. It's time to throw ourselves a life preserver, while there is still a ship to get back on.

It all comes down to four little words that can save the day, the country, the world, and our souls. Say them. Wear them. Shout them. Explain them.

38

VOTE 4 FOR ALL

VOTE 4 For All!

This can become the greatest moment in human history. We have gloriously reached the point that there really is enough of everything to go around. It is truly a triumph, and we must begin believing and treating it as such. For the first time in our bloody savage history, we have no need to fight with each other for resources. Enough exists that we can all live safely and comfortably. It is all so ridiculously **doable**. We are literally at the doorstep of our most grand accomplishment as a species. We need only believe it, ask for it, and settle for nothing less.

VOTE 4 For All!

NOT FOOTNOTES
SOME NOTES ABOUT NOTES THAT AREN'T FOOTNOTES

After giving it some thought, I decided not to use footnotes in this book. I'm pretty sure Strunk & White would back me up on this, but they were unavailable for comment. The main reason is that nobody ever reads them anyway. I know I don't and that's plenty reason enough.

That's not to say that there wasn't research. There was. A lot of it. Dozens of hours and literally thousands of statistics. Part of my research was done using the very first, primitive, but shiny new ChatGPT. I am quite sure that anything I might have to say on this subject will age poorly, but I found it to be a reasonably good research tool. Except for when it told me that California was bigger in land mass than Texas. I'm not kidding.

For the record, at no time did I rely solely on AI for any of the research in this book. Multiple sources were used to zero in on reliable statistics and study results.

Here's the ChatGPT exchange:

D

is Texas bigger than California?

ChatGPT

No, California is larger than Texas in terms of land area. California is the largest state in the United States by land area, covering approximately 423,970 square kilometers (163,696 square miles). In contrast, Texas is the second-largest state, with a land area of about 695,660 square kilometers (268,581 square miles). So, California is bigger than Texas when it comes to land area.

D

I think you are confused. the numbers seemed to show Texas as bigger.

ChatGPT

Apologies for the confusion. You are correct. Texas is indeed larger than California in terms of land area. I apologize for the incorrect information in my previous response.

Texas is the second-largest state in the United States, covering approximately 695,660 square kilometers (268,581 square miles). California, on the other hand, is the third-largest state, with a land area of about 423,970 square kilometers (163,696 square miles).

Thank you for pointing out the mistake. and I apologize for any confusion caused.

If you took the time to read that, you might note that it also told me that California is not only bigger than Texas but the biggest state in the U.S. by land mass. Which would also make it bigger than Alaska. Um, no. We got it all straightened out eventually, but I think it's fair to say we should be wary of AI.

Also, what you see above is the **only** time that I used any AI results verbatim. The reason for that is, I think, extremely important. I believe anything produced by AI is, by its very nature, plagiarism. AI is the sum of everything, and *everyone* fed into it. The words it scours were at some time the words and work of **someone**. That work, for better or worse, will always belong to its original author. Even if that author thought that California is bigger than Texas.

AUTHOR'S NOTES, ACKNOWLEDGEMENTS, AND RANDOM THOUGHTS

I'd like to think of this book as a recipe to save the world. As such, it will break a record for the use of the word "fuck" in a cookbook.

I tried to understand what a world without fear of need would look like, and in doing so ask you to understand what this world could be. It really is possible. We really can do it.

Despite a couple hundred pages of evidence to the contrary, I am not delusional. I know the odds are very much against both this book and the world.

I know that even just the odds of this book being widely read are a couple of million to one. And I think even that is probably overly optimistic. It makes me think of the still great movie *Dumb and Dumber* where Jim Carrey's character says, "So you're saying there is a chance." Brilliant stuff, the very existence of which sometimes brings me hope. In the same way as listening to side two of The Beatles' *Abbey Road* album. That there are some people that can create such breathtaking beauty and brilliance always gives me this slender ray of hope. And here's to you, Wes Anderson.

And at least I can say I tried.

As I begin the process of checking out from Hotel Earth, I will do so knowing that I gave it a shot in the only way I know how. Especially since other ways of helping might involve getting my hands, or honor, dirty. Or even worse, cause me to go somewhere cold for more than twenty minutes.

And because I seem to be making this into something of a pre-obituary, I want to tell anyone in the world to whom it may matter the following message: I DO NOT FORGIVE YOU. Not because I am holding a grudge or any lingering bad will. No, it's because it doesn't even remotely matter if I forgive you or not. You don't need my forgiveness and do not deserve my attention enough to warrant my wrath.

Nor do I seek forgiveness from anyone, for much the same reason. I know one thing for certain. I have never gone out of my way to hurt anyone. A point that was driven home to me recently by a disturbing series of events. Where I found people that were very, very happy to harm me. Literally giddy about it. Did I deserve it? I don't know. They certainly seemed to think so. In that circumstance, I had ample opportunity to get in a few shots of my own, and I very nearly did.

But I successfully delayed my reaction, reminding myself that the opportunity to act out of spite would still be available the next day. And during the process of deciding against taking actions out of spite, I realized and remembered that I have NEVER actually done so. I have never deliberately hurt someone. And after this series of events, I think it's safe to say I never will. Believe me, if there was ever a time to be spiteful, this was it.

And that's not to say that I have never hurt anyone. I know that I've done more than my fair share of stupid things. There were more than enough times where I would have been better off keeping my mouth shut, but I never set out to purposefully harm anyone. And these recent events also helped me to realize why I don't hurt people and the reason, it turns out, is actually quite selfish. I simply will not allow these happily mean-spirited people to turn me into them. I will not permit them to turn me into a person that acts out of spite. That remains my choice. For better or for worse, I get to go on being me. For a little while yet anyway. And they will continue to be them. That, I think, is justice defined.

I cannot forget the contribution of my friend Jeff Jabick, LMHC. If somehow this shit actually turns into something, we will all owe Jeff a debt of gratitude. His input at the exact right time is almost enough to make me believe that there is some kind of order to this chaos. This book might not exist without you, Jeff. Thanks!

And the former Linda Litvin, you are the kindest person I have ever known. None of this happens without your kindness and support. Even when I didn't deserve it.

Here's something that I kept looking for a relevant place to say. I couldn't quite find one, so let's put it here. It might now be relevant. I think I made it up, but who knows? Maybe I read it somewhere and just forgot. Here goes:

"Inspiration without perspiration is masturbation." I love it. And the point, in case you missed it, is this: Ideas alone are worthless. Everyone has ideas. Unless you really do something with an idea, you are just jerking off.

Last thing. I would like to offer a tip of my hat to the thirty-sixth President of the United States, Lyndon Johnson. I have few personal heroes, and he is one of them. He was a complicated man with a complicated legacy. But one thing is for certain: Without Johnson, there is no Civil Rights Act of 1964, one, if not the single most important, step in the right direction. Johnson was a Texan, and a southerner through and through. But he was strong enough to rise above the sea of bias and hatred he was born into, and he knew that this bold step would cost him politically. No one knew better than he did the political cost of doing what he knew was right. Talking about his party, he said, "We have lost the South for a generation" and "We have just delivered the South to the Republican Party for a long time." And of course, he was right. Racist Democrats of the South rushed to join their racist Republican colleagues who stood firmly in the way of civic freedom and progress. Those same forces remain. And it is not an overstatement to say that it is this that keeps millions voting against their own interests to this day. Today they may call it something else, but it is racism that still aligns them with those who buy and sell our country and our world.

Well, now that we settled that, let's get out there and save the world. Well, not the world exactly. The earth will go on just fine with or without us. So when I say, "Get out there and save the world," what I really mean is "Get out there and save *us*." Save our species, our people, our country. *Why the Fuck Not?* Why are you still here? Go!

If you want to contact me so you can tell me all the things I fucked up, please do. I can be reached at Dlkosmo@gmail.com or check out DavidLitvin.com to see my novels and god knows what else.

ABOUT THE AUTHOR

David Litvin has spent most of his adult life in two worlds. The first was in the Basque sport of Jai Alai. He was the U.S National Amateur Jai-Alai champion in 1990. He played jai alai in the Campeonato De Mundial (World Championship) in Havana, Cuba, as part of the Pan American Games. As a representative of the United States, a fourth-place finish earned the U.S. a berth in the 1992 Olympic Games in Barcelona, Spain. Later, his attention turned to the world of poker where he was a profitable, professional player and later a poker dealer, poker tournament director, and poker room director.

His previous work is a musical stage play about the world of high stakes poker, *All In: The Poker Musical,* which featured original songs by Grammy award winner Vini Poncia.

He tries to keep his needs simple and his masters few.

THE AUTHOR MAY BE REACHED AT:

DLKOSMO@GMAIL.COM OR

DAVIDLITVIN.COM

ALSO BY DAVID L. LITVIN

Silencer's End

The Monochrome Solution

Frum God: The Mostly True Adventures of a Modern Day Messiah

All In: The Poker Musical

www.ingramcontent.com/pod-product-compliance
Lightning Source LLC
Chambersburg PA
CBHW072211150726
48002CB00005B/1757